The Part Time War

For my wife Vi, who deciphered my unintelligible writing, and Sue and Mike who, as children, waved goodbye to me on every call-up.

The Part Time War

Recollections of the Terrorist War in Rhodesia 1975–78

Rod Wells

Illustrations by the author

Fern House

First published in 2011 by
Fern House, Haddenham, Cambridgeshire CB6 3XA
www.fernhouse.com

ISBN-13 978–1–902702–25–4

Jacket design: Vi Wells
Layout: istudio21, Cambridge
Printing: QNS, Newcastle upon Tyne

CONTENTS

EASTERN DISTRICTS

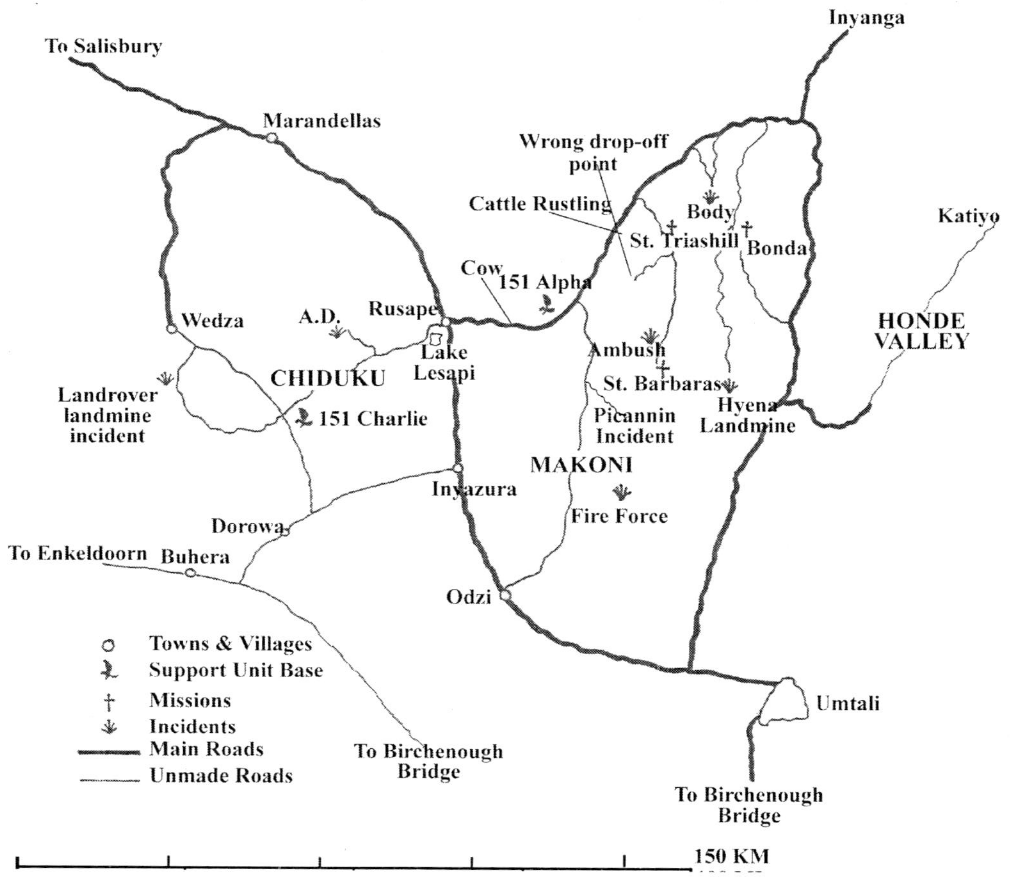

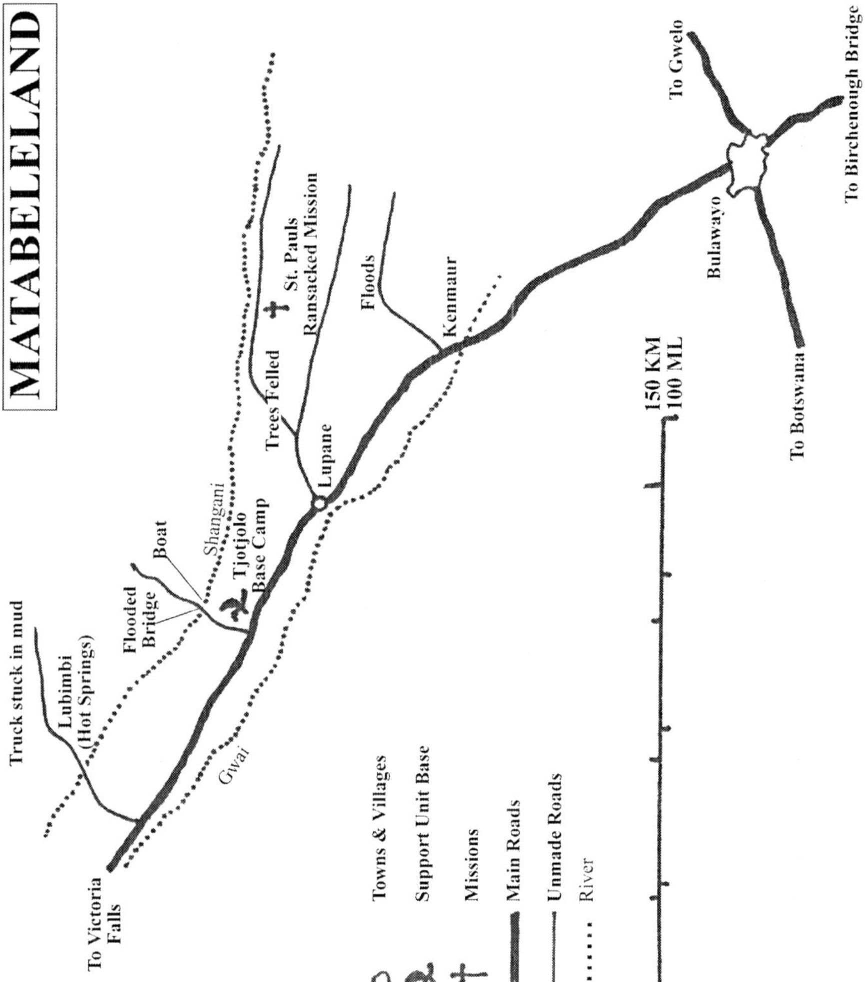
MATABELELAND
Truck stuck in mud
Lubimbi (Hot Springs)
Flooded Bridge
Boat
Shangani
Tjotjolo Base Camp
Trees Felled
St. Pauls Ransacked Mission
Floods
Lupane
Kenmaur
Gwai
To Victoria Falls
Bulawayo
To Gwelo
To Birchenough Bridge
To Botswana
150 KM
100 ML
Towns & Villages
Support Unit Base
Missions
Main Roads
Unmade Roads
River

RHODESIA

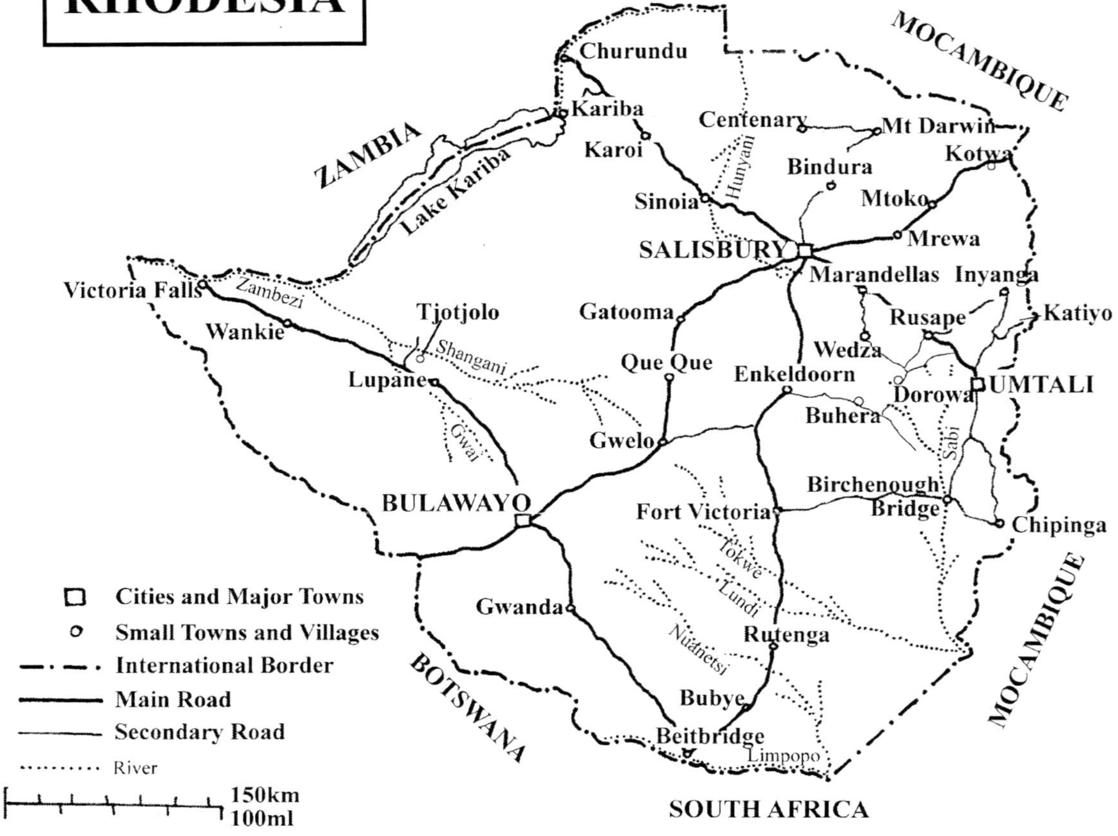

After independence in 1980, many place names were changed if they did not relate to the local dialect or had colonial connotations. The map has Rhodesian names that are referred to in this book but the table below shows the Zimbabwe equivalent.

Rhodesia	Zimbabwe
Salisbury	Harare
Sinioa	Chinhoyi
Marandellas	Marondera
Inyanga	Nyanga
Umtali	Mutare
Chipinga	Chipinge
Fort Victoria	Masvingo
Enkeldoorn	Chivhu
Gatooma	Kadoma
Que Que	Kwekwe
Gwelo	Gweru
Wankie	Hwange

Abbreviations and Vernacular Words

AD	Accidental discharge. When a firearm is fired by accident.
AK	A light assault rifle invented by Anatol Kolashnikov used by the terrorists.
CPU	Coloured Protection Unit. Mixed race men, armed to protect road maintenance gangs, bridges, electrical installations, etc.
DA	District Assistant. An African employed by the Internal Affairs department carrying out administrative duties in the country districts.
FN	Fabrique Nationale. A Belgium made rifle issued to most members of the security forces.
FRELIMO	Frente de Libertaçao de Mocambique. Liberation front of Mocambique.
INTAF	Internal Affairs government department looking after the administration of the country districts.
JOC	Joint Operations Centre, usually placed at a police station or army camp.
LOC	Location by latitude and longditude.
MAG	Heavy machine gun used by the Rhodesian security forces.
OP	Observation Post.
PATU	Police Anti Terrorist Unit. Specialist tracking unit.
RAR	Rhodesian African Rifles. An African army regiment.

RLI	Rhodesian Light Infantry.
RPD	A communist light machine gun.
SAS	Special Air Service similar to the British SAS.
SMG	Sub machine gun. Usually an Uzi
TTL	Tribal Trust Land. African common land similar to American Indian reservation.
TILCOR	Tribal Trust Land Development Corporation has a number of agricultural projects in the TTLs.
UZI	Sub-machine gun of Israeli design.
ZANU	Zimbabwe African National Union. A banned political party mainly backed by the Shona tribes.
ZAPU	Zimbabwe African Peoples Union. A banned political party mainly backed by the Ndebele tribes.
ZANLA	Zimbabwe African National Liberation Army. The military wing of ZANU.
ZIPRA	Zimbabwe Peoples Republican Army. The military wing of ZAPU.
Bedford RM	A 4 wheel drive Bedford MK but always referred to in Rhodesia as an RM.
Gomo	A local word for a large granite topped hill.
Kopje	A small hill.
Koeksisters	An Afrikaans snack similar to a light doughnut.
Kraal	An African village pronounced 'crawl'.
Picannin	An African child.
Ters	Short for terrorist, sometimes called gooks.
Veldt	Open, thinly wooded country, also spelled veld.
Voetsak	An Afrikaans explanation meaning go away or I don't believe you. Closest English meaning is bugger off or worse.
Vlei	Marshland.

Introduction

This is the true story of an ordinary person unwittingly caught up in a terrorist war. It is a story of Rhodesia in the nineteen seventies when the African Nationalists were fighting for independence from the white-dominated government.

As the war intensified, all able-bodied men were called up to serve in the various branches of the security forces. At that time, I was running a small garage business and my wife and I had a young family. The inevitable call up papers arrived and the story starts to unfold.

There are no tales of incredible heroics or daily skirmishes. There is action but, like all wars, there are also hours of idleness and moments of great tension as we sought out the terrorist groups while they moved through the countryside. There are, however, tales of humour, hilarity, seriousness, horror and sadness.

I have tried not to put a political slant on my writings but to put over my feelings as events took place before my eyes. I saw injustices committed by both sides but, unless one has been involved in a conflict like this, it cannot be compared to the common justice of everyday life in the western world. Life was and still is very hard in Africa and I witnessed incidents and events that I felt I had to put down on paper.

I have had to depend on my memory for the names of the many people I met during this time but no names have been deliberately changed and all place names are as they were known before independence. When vernacular words or abbreviations are used they are explained in the text or in the heading list. All weights and measurements are shown in metric form because Rhodesia metricated totally in the early nineteen seventies.

These memoirs cover the years from 1975 to 1978, after the government, led by Prime Minister Ian Smith, had conceded to handing over to African majority rule. It was naïvely thought that the nationalist leaders would return for talks and the conflict cease but, unfortunately, the war gradually intensified as those leaders fought for supremacy. Hopes were dashed that out of the conflict the various parties could come to an agreement which would give an independent Rhodesia a stable government with an integrated multiracial society to head towards a strong economy to benefit the whole population.

After 1975 the security forces were stretched to the limit in maintaining some semblance of order to enable the peaceful hand-over to independence that finally came in 1980.

Unfortunately, over the ensuing years, events have overtaken the country to dash the aspirations and dreams of so many well meaning people within and without the country that is now known as Zimbabwe.

Rod Wells
Cambridge, England,
October 2010

CHAPTER 1

Conscription

The eight by four inch white patch in the centre of the target, one hundred yards away, appeared no bigger than a pinhead as I lined up the sights on my FN, automatic, high velocity rifle.

"From a prone position, fire five rounds in your own time."

"Face the target - Fire!"

Gently I squeezed the trigger and, for a split second, the weapon was alive as it barked in my hands. A spent cartridge case spat out as the butt kicked back to bruise my cheek. With careful aim I fired off the remaining four rounds and then laid the rifle down, hands shaking slightly as the adrenaline coursed through my veins.

No longer having to focus upon the target ahead I relaxed, my gaze wandering along the line of prone, camouflaged figures stretching across the firing range. Beneath the battle dress there lay an odd assortment of doctors, accountants, clerks, farmers, salesmen and, in my case, a motor mechanic. Ages ranged from early twenties to late fifties. What on earth were we doing here? This being a situation so different from our normal, molycoddled, eight-to-five existences. The answer lay in the fact that this was Rhodesia in 1976.

The terrorist war, which had started as no more than a border skirmish, had spread like a cancer, gradually inflicting its disease on the civil life of the country.

The first notable incident, back in December 1972, was an attack on an isolated farmhouse in the Centenary area, North East of Salisbury, within forty miles of the Mozambique border. The police and army tried to track down the culprits but this was to be just the first of many such attacks and incursions. 'Operation Hurricane', as it was to be designated, had begun and would become one of the hottest areas of the ensuing war.

The manpower needed for defence increased in direct proportion to the number of terrorist incidents. It was estimated that for each and every terrorist in the country, a minimum of one hundred members of the security forces were involved, ranging from trackers and soldiers to office personnel.

At first, the terrorist incidents were treated as criminal offences, with the police taking a leading role, using the army as a back up. However, as the number of incidents increased, so the army took more responsibility, until a system of joint operations was established between the army, air force and police. A network of Joint Operations Centres (JOC) was set up at strategic points throughout the country, under the overall command of the army, to co-ordinate anti-terrorist operations. A JOC would consist of an operations room equipped with a powerful radio transmitter, sometimes based close to a police station or airfield, but normally incorporated as part of a large army camp.

The security forces at that time consisted of the Army, with a number of battalions, including the Rhodesian Light Infantry (RLI), Rhodesia African Rifles (RAR) the Special Air Service (SAS) and a large contingent of Territorials. The Rhodesian Air Force carried out its duties in a similar fashion to air forces throughout the world, at that time being equipped with Vampire Jets, Hawker Hunters, Canberra bombers and Alouette helicopters. The British South Africa Police force (the title of which is a misnomer as it had nothing to do with Britain or South Africa), in addition to carrying out the normal uniformed duties of any police force, had a large number of volunteers, called B Reserve, trained in riot control, particularly active in the country areas where farmers and locals could back up the small local police presence. In addition, there was the Police Anti-Terrorist Unit (PATU) and Support Unit.

PATU was a highly trained unit which sent out a small number of men, normally five or six and known as a 'stick', who were well trained in bush craft and whose job was to track down insurgents.

Support Unit was a para-military unit of African policemen, originally known as Askaris and all regulars. The unit was run on strict military lines and had its own barracks and administration centre.

As the war intensified, even more specialised units were created. The army formed the crack tracker unit, the Selous Scouts and the mounted Grey's Scouts. With the increased commitment of the mixed race community, the Coloured Protection Unit (CPU) was formed for the defence of road works, maintenance gangs and vulnerable installations like dams, electricity sub-stations and the like.

The Police vastly increased the size of its reserve force and also formed a mounted tracker unit which was seconded to the Support Unit.

In addition to all these various units, the Internal Affairs Department of the Government decided to create its own armed force for the defence and protection of its own personnel, who were scattered around the country trying to carry out normal civil administrative affairs.

To confuse matters even further, a Guard Force was then set up to protect anyone who wasn't already protected - if there were any? So many of these units overlapped that it was surprising that they didn't end up shooting at each other.

Despite National Service never having been discontinued in Rhodesia I, through no deliberate fault of my own, had avoided a commitment until 1976. When I had been first called up in 1962, as an eighteen year old, I had reported for my medical examination with some trepidation. I was fit and active, so I was therefore very surprised to be designated to Category C and told my services were not required. Ironically, at the same time, a close friend, who had lost his index finger in a carpentry accident, was passed fit and as a rifleman to boot! Still, who was I to complain? The country was very peaceful at that time, although the Belgian Congo had erupted into violence and the Federation of Rhodesia and Nyasaland was close to break up. With typical adolescent lack of vision I was enjoying life and was glad not to have an army commitment.

In 1965 came the infamous Unilateral Declaration of Independence (UDI) and the whole world recoiled in horror retaliating, with the help of the United Nations, by applying trade sanctions. However, even without official world trade, day by day life changed little, that is, until 1972. After that first terrorist act, things were never to be the same again. Unfelt at first, slowly but surely, the lives of all Rhodesians, black and white, were to change irreversibly.

As the war escalated, so the requirement for more manpower increased and soon exceeded the available regular and territorial forces. More manpower had to be sourced from the working male population. However, to finance the war, the economy of the country had to be maintained and those who would now be required to fight were also needed to keep the economy going.

A natural compromise arose and we therefore became a nation of part time soldiers, spending up to a maximum of one hundred and eighty days per year in the security forces and the remainder of the year at our normal jobs. However, at first, only those men who had completed their initial National Service and were still under 30 years old were called up in this net, so I escaped once again.

Although the war was being waged less than 120 kilometres from Salisbury, the capital, every day life was so peaceful that the conflict seemed to be in another world. Content with my family and business life I felt only slightly guilty as the call up net once again failed to envelope me.

My wife and I had set up a small garage business in 1971 which had evolved successfully and complemented my hobby of motor racing, which I campaigned successfully in a production car formula, culminating in winning a Rhodesian National Championship in 1974 and 1975. The last thing I needed at this time of my life was time off work at the Government's pleasure.

My complacency was short-lived however and, one day in 1974, I received a communication from the Ministry of Defence ordering me to attend a medical examination at the King George V Barracks. The age limit for conscription had recently been raised to thirty and all those who, for whatever reason, had not completed military training were being examined and, when pronounced fit, drafted into the army for three months basic training.

I duly presented myself at the barrack hospital and joined a queue of indifferent looking individuals, amongst whom I recognised some acquaintances from the Motor Trade and Motor Sport. While we waited, various nervous jokes were cracked about Dads Army and we were amused at the variety of obscure ailments that were being dug up and put on the medical forms. Weak backs, flat feet and migraines topped the list. I wished that I had been told exactly what had kept me out of the armed forces all those years ago, when I was eighteen, as I had nothing of any consequence to put on my form.

Slowly the queue moved forward until a tight lipped corporal blocked my way. With barely a flicker of interest he checked my form against a master list and then handed the form back, plus a small bottle.

Rejoining the queue I slowly shuffled along to a couple of cubicles. It was here that I found that I was one of those who find it difficult to pee whilst being watched. It didn't matter what I did or thought, that little bottle remained dry. The feet in the next cubicle were changing with the monotony of a production line, whilst my queue was stuck fast, waiting for me.

From behind came cries of, "Hurry up."

"What's the hold up?"

"Perhaps he can't find it," some jester cracked.

With a sweating brow I eventually managed a dribble in the bottom of the bottle and rejoined the exit line. Everyone else appeared to be carrying a pint of light ale as opposed to my single whiskey and, self-consciously, I handed my dregs to the medical orderly. The rest of the medical continued without a hitch until I came to the last doctor.

"I see from your medical history that you have a deformed left hand!"

For a moment I stood nonplussed, assuming the doctor was reading from the wrong form, then suddenly I remembered the childhood accident which had left me with a stunted little finger and weak grip. It had never given me any particular problems or interfered with my work. I certainly didn't consider it a disability but it was something that had to be noted on the medical form.

Seizing hold of the offending object he said, "Squeeze my hand."

Without realising the implication I squeezed his hand as tightly as I could. I was tempted to crush this man's fingers - how dare he say that I was deformed.

"Yes, that's definitely weak," he stated.

"But I'm right handed," I gasped, in indignation, not realising the implication of failing the medical examination.

"Maybe, but you couldn't lug a rifle around all day with that hand," came the reply and before I knew it I was outside, blinking in the sunshine, finding it hard to believe that I had been given a reprieve. I had been rejected yet again.

Over the next few months the war escalated fast and I began to get my first tinges of guilt at not doing anything for the war effort. Most of my friends had some sort of commitment and those that didn't had genuine medical reasons for not doing so. Despite the doctor picking out my weak left hand, in reality there really was no reason for me not to do my bit.

I hadn't long to feel guilty, however, as within a year another buff coloured envelope dropped through my letter box. The words 'On Government Service' and 'Ministry of Defence' leapt from the cover. I opened it and saw the fateful words 'You will report to ......' There were none of the niceties of civilian life. They couldn't say 'please' or ' you are requested,' just a straightforward 'You will' and no messing about.

Reading on, I found that I was required to report to the Internal Affairs training ground at Chikurubi – a village near Salisbury that gained notoriety after independence as a detention centre with a very harsh regime - in October 1975 for an initial training period of three months, prior to my first territorial call up period of six weeks.

My heart sank as I read what was the worst possible news I could have received. The reasons were three fold. First and foremost, my wife Vi was eight months pregnant with our second child and as she was to have a Caesarean section I would be needed to look after our two and a half year old daughter Susan. Not only while Vi was in hospital but for some time after her return home. Second, I had staff on army commitment as well, so I would have no option but to close my business down if I was away for any length of time. Third, the last group I wished to be called up with was Internal Affairs, because INTAF was not a fighting force, but purely a government administration defence force.

The defence force consisted almost entirely of men like me who had escaped the call-up net but whose lower grades of physical fitness were quite acceptable for the duties required of them. The main duty was the manning of the many forts that had been constructed from earth and wood and were scattered throughout the country, looking like Anglo-Saxon stockades incongruously transplanted into the African veldt.

Alongside some of these forts, protected villages had been built. These were enormous areas enclosed by a perimeter security fence, including a lookout tower, into which the local populace were moved en bloc without option. The theory being that, with a secure village, the local population would be free from intimidation and the terrorists would be denied sanctuary. Without local co-operation it was thought that the terrorists would find it hard to exist. A theory gleaned from the experience of the British Army in Malaya in the 1950s. Unfortunately, it did not work so well in practise, because these protected villages became branded as concentration camps in anti-government propaganda.

From the forts, the African District Assistants (DA) would go about their administrative duties armed with ancient .303 rifles, dating from the Second World War. The INTAF conscript had to spend approximately four call ups of six weeks duration each year cooped up in one of these forts, many miles from anywhere, often having no company, other than the DAs for the full six weeks. The DAs were a specific target of the terrorists because they were regarded as being the link between raw Africa and government authority. Without that link the countryside would succumb to anarchy and confusion. Consequently, there were weekly reports of DAs being murdered. Although armed, they were no match for a terrorist group armed with AK47 automatic rifles. The forts often came under attack although, due to the design and the fact that they were generally attacked at night by ill trained groups, fatalities were low.

As I didn't fancy the prospect of being a sitting duck I decided to set in motion the first steps to get out of my INTAF commitment. If I had got to go, I wanted to do something better than this.

First of all I applied for a deferment on compassionate grounds until the new baby was home and settled. The powers that be were not unsympathetic and this was easily obtained, with a three month deferment being allowed. I then applied to the Exemption Board asking for a hearing to discuss a transfer to a different unit where, hopefully, I might not be away from my business for such long periods of time. The Board had the power to refuse a hearing, so after a worrying few weeks I was very relieved to receive a letter from them granting a hearing in January 1976. In the meantime I armed myself with as much data as possible to put the case that the future of my business and my employees was at stake.

The day of the interview arrived and it was a good thirty minutes before the allotted time that, with nerves tingling, I parked in the shade of the jacaranda trees outside the District Commissioner's Office. With a feeling of slight nausea, I sat in the austere corridor with one other applicant, a medical student, who was trying to avoid disruption to his training. He was called in after a few minutes, leaving me with my own thoughts. I flicked through a few dog eared magazines uncomprehendingly. After half an hour the student reappeared grim faced.

"Bastards," he hissed as he strode out of the building. My heart sank into my boots as he obviously hadn't received the result that he had hoped for. My carefully thought out reasons for a transfer suddenly seemed rather pathetic compared that of a medical student. My pondering was interrupted by a call. "Mister Wells come this way please," I rose to meet my fate.

Entering the boardroom I was shown to a solitary, straight backed chair facing a semi-circle of humourless figures. The chairman introduced himself and immediately the ball was thrown into my court. Leaning forward, he said, "Would you explain your reasons and circumstances as to why we should exempt you from your call-up commitment with the Internal Affairs department."

As I heard myself starting to state my position both from a personal and business point of view there was not the slightest sign of either emotion or interest on the faces before me. Undaunted, I plodded on. When I had finished, a few questions were asked and then they conferred in low voices. After a few minutes the Chairman spoke. "We, as a Board, have no power to transfer you from your commitment as laid down under the Manpower Act, neither have you given good cause for exemption."

I sat listening miserably as his words dully penetrated my brain. Then suddenly I realised what he was inferring.

"However, we will grant you a six month deferment to enable you to reorganise your affairs so that you are available for training," then, with the first signs of understanding in his eyes, he added. "Unofficially, I suggest that during this six months you volunteer for Police Reserve duty. On your being accepted by them we would no longer feel obliged to require your services."

In a daze I spluttered out my thanks, left the room and drove the few blocks to the Morris Police Depot where I was soon filling in an application form. My journey into the Rhodesian Security Forces had begun.

BRITISH SOUTH AFRICA POLICE

CHAPTER 2

Initial Training

An advantage of being in the Police Reserve was that the call-up system was flexible and consequently more favourable for businessmen. The annual commitment in 1976 was 56 days, compared to 120 days in the other services and these were divided into four call ups of 14 days duration. Deferments were easier to obtain so I had hopes of our business continuing albeit under difficult conditions. It was with some relief, therefore, that I received my next buff envelope, this time franked with the words 'Police Reserve', containing my acceptance into the force.

I was now officially Number 23321Y Field Reservist Wells R.E.J. assigned to Golf section - this being the phonetic code name for section G - not some sports division.

Shortly afterwards I received a communication from Section Leader Martin inviting me to attend the monthly briefing at the Police Reserve pub. Definitely a more civilised approach than the 'You will' of the army and INTAF.

I duly arrived at the pub and, after searching through the milling throngs lining the bar like battery hens, eventually found Golf section tucked away in a corner. On making myself known I was met with a friendly welcome and introduced to the members present. The next couple of hours were spent listening to past escapades whilst imbibing a few jars of beer. It became evident that the only official dealings I would have with the authorities would be notifications of call ups and training days. I was on my own so far as orientating myself and finding my feet in this new escapade. This meeting therefore was very helpful in finding out about kit, where various stores, offices and armoury were and who to report to. I left the meeting relieved to be placed with such a helpful and friendly group and keen to get stuck in.

The next week I procured a chit to take to the Quartermaster's store and it was with some wry humour that I presented my 6 foot 6 inch frame to the orderly behind the counter. Not only am I tall, but my feet match my height and I was very intrigued to see if they had a pair of size 13 boots in stock.

The expressionless African orderly measured me up and my amusement changed to astonishment when a uniform and twolarge black boots were plonked down on the counter before me.

"Try these on," came the bored command. Dubiously I entered the changing cubicle and on trying on the shirt and trousers found that, if anything, they were on the large side. Self consciously I shuffled out and sheepishly said. "A bit too big I think."

"They'll shrink," came the curt reply, as the remaining kit was ticked off by the humourless issuing officer.

Amongst the kit was a khaki web belt and anklets. These, I was informed, must be blacked to comply with the regulations. A close friend of mine told me of an old army trick: apply black boot polish liberally on the webbing and then pass the flame of a candle over to melt the polish into the material. That evening saw me in my workshop with a new tin of Nugget. I deftly applied the polish and, to speed up the operation, instead of using a candle I struck up a low flame on the oxy-acetylene equipment. All went well and I soon had an immaculate set of black webbing but I was sure that just one more application was needed to make them perfect. Full of confidence, by now, I flashed the torch once more across the belt when, to my horror, the liquefied polish ignited. Frantically I blew at it, but to no avail and ended up throwing it onto the floor and stamping on the fire in my panic. Within seconds my immaculate belt had transformed into a smouldering mess. On closer inspection however, other than a few charred edges, the webbing appeared to be intact but all the stitching had disintegrated. The remainder of the evening was spent salvaging the remnants with needle and cotton.

I had been informed at the briefing that the police training was very basic and that I should take advantage of the various voluntary training clinics available. Naturally my first thought was weapon training and the next Saturday morning found me sitting with half a dozen other recruits at the Morris Depot awkwardly holding an FN automatic rifle in my lap. Just the feeling of the weight and the cold, finely machined steel was exciting and I began to understand why just this feeling brings out a natural aggression, a basic animal instinct our forebears felt who had to fight and hunt for survival.

Over the next few hours we were taught the principals of an automatic rifle - how it worked, how to strip, adjust and load it and, most importantly, the safety precautions.

"Never point a weapon unless you intend to use it. Don't play games, even though you know it's unloaded. There is no more pathetic plea than, "I didn't know it was loaded," after you've shot your mate," cautioned the instructor.

With excited anticipation we clambered aboard a Land Rover for the short journey to the small shooting range behind the parade ground.

Three cardboard targets were erected and the ammunition divided out, just 10 rounds per person.

"Load the magazine with five rounds," came the order. We did so, then three of us self consciously stood facing the targets, the rifle held in the right hand by the pistol grip, the barrel pointing skywards. With the magazine clasped in our left hand, we waited in trepidation for the next command.

"Fit the magazine."

With fumbling fingers we clipped in the magazine.

"Cock your weapons."

Our hands now sweating and being unfamiliar with the feel of the rifle, all three of us jammed the first round. The person on my left looked back enquiringly at the instructor.

"Don't turn round," came the urgent shout from behind. "Stay where you are and face the target."

"Remove the magazine."

We complied.

"Cock your rifle again."

This cleared the breech.

"Refit the magazine, and this time, when I say cock, pull the lever bloody hard and then let go in one movement. Don't play with it, get physical." We went back to square one and this time cocked successfully.

"When I give the command, take aim and fire all five rounds in your own time."

We waited expectantly, hands trembling from the tension. The mere fact that this powerful weapon was ready to fire, and could potentially kill, caused the nerves to tingle.

"Fire!"

Lifting the butt to my shoulder I squinted along the barrel trying to line up the sights but to no avail as I was shaking violently. Taking a few deep breaths I tried again. As the sights shook across the target I pulled the trigger. With a deafening report the barrel jerked upwards and the butt recoiled sharply back into my shoulder. I unleashed the remaining four rounds and then stood back trembling, ears ringing from the thunderous explosions.

Laying our rifles down, we moved forward and inspected the targets. The cardboard figure I had been aiming at had four punctures; one round had missed completely. We affixed paper patches to the target to repair the damage and stood back to watch the remaining trainees. They fared no better and soon it was our turn again. This time all five of my rounds found the target, although at only 25 yards, this was hardly impressive shooting.

Afterwards as we sat cleaning our rifles, with the traditional 4 x 2 inch cloth and pull through, I mentioned my nervousness to the instructor. He laughed, "Nothing unusual about that, most people have that reaction when first handed a high velocity rifle like an FN, you'll be all right next time."

He was proved correct when just two weeks later I reported for an official training day. I joined a motley collection of men self consciously wearing new and ill fitting uniforms. We were herded into the lecture hall adjoining the parade ground where I sat with anticipation. Now I was in I wanted to get on with things.

First there was a short briefing on the state of the war at that time and our role within the overall situation. Then the training started. The first lecture was on map reading. Unfortunately the instructor was more concerned with the correct way of folding the map than with the interpretation of the works thereon. After an hour of folding and unfolding we hadn't grasped much in the art of map reading, but we were certainly proficient in the art of map folding. Fortunately, I wasn't too perturbed as I had done quite a bit of motor rallying in the past, where map reading is essential in following a route, so that didn't matter too much as far as I was concerned.

Next came a lecture on counter vehicle ambush procedure. Diagrams were drawn on a blackboard with such delightful areas described as 'the killing zone' and 'the angle of fire'. The types of ambush situation were described to us and then it boiled down to using our eyes and ears. I learnt that when the firing started under no circumstances to panic – easy to say in the classroom – or to stop but to keep going unless the road was blocked because a moving target is - so we were told - relatively hard to hit. Although I didn't know it at the time, this was to be the most important lecture of all and would possibly be responsible for saving me from injury or worse.

Appropriately, the next lecture was on first aid. In the middle of all this masculinity we were confronted by an extremely attractive nursing sister, who was greeted with wolf whistles and a few ribald comments. Unperturbed, she started off by describing the types of situations and wounds that we might be confronted with. She demonstrated how to deal with burns, wounds, bleeding, broken limbs and shock. When asked for volunteers to demonstrate on, chairs were knocked aside in the mad scramble to get close to this perfumed beauty but when it came to artificial respiration, a groan of disappointment could be heard when she produced a dummy on which to demonstrate mouth to mouth resuscitation. She got her own back on us though, and had us blushing with embarrassment, when she recommended that we carry a packet of tampons with us as they are particularly well adapted to plugging gunshot wounds and stemming the flow of blood. To illustrate the point a gruesome film of actual casualties followed, "Just to show you what you may be faced with." As the last frames flickered to the end we rose and, feeling slightly nauseous, filed out into the fresh air where, for a moment, I thought our recently acquired knowledge was going to be put to good use when a huge Afrikaans farmer emerged with a grey complexion, swaying visibly, into the bright sunlight.

In any war involving rough terrain and few good roads, helicopters are a necessity. As we would all come up against this form of transport at some time or another it was necessary to be trained in the correct procedure to be adopted when boarding such a craft.

Our 'helicopter' consisted of a group of wooden chairs laid out in the centre of the parade square. We took it in turns to be pilot, gunner and passengers and soon we were attracting a great deal of attention from the office block. Some participants threw themselves enthusiastically into the roles using appropriate noises, not unlike children playing at cowboys and indians.

Soon the morning had gone and, after a quick lunch, we each drew a rifle and two magazines from the armoury and waited for the arrival of transport to take us to a nearby rifle range. We were slightly surprised when this transport turned out to be two grey prison trucks, fitted with wooden seats, mesh grill windows and 'Prison Service' painted prominently on the sides. When the driver then proceeded to take us right through the city centre there was a mad scramble to pull down the canvas window screens and we finished the journey incognito in the dimness within.

After debussing at the range we were formed into two columns. One column marched off to the butts to operate and patch the targets whilst the rest of us were issued with fifty rounds of ammunition. As we lined up across the range at the 100 yard mark, we saw twenty targets raised and as I was fourth from the right, I presumed that I was to fire at target number 17. What I hadn't realised was that when we divided into two columns we didn't have equal numbers, one column contained twenty people, but mine contained only nineteen. We shot off our preliminary five rounds and walked up to the target to inspect our work. Mine was totally unmarked and I was feeling rather nonplussed, because I was sure that I was a better shot than that, when I heard an exclamation to my right. "I've got ten holes in mine!" The truth dawned on me, I was in a group of nineteen and should have been firing at target 16, not 17. Sheepishly I informed the instructor of my mistake and, with eighteen pairs of eyes on me, I reloaded and fired off five more rounds, this time forming a tight grouping on my target.

My only previous experience of handling a firearm was as a teenager when I roamed the bush with the inevitable air rifle terrorising defenceless sparrows. I had been quite a good shot then and I was pleased that I seemed to be getting my eye in again.

Adjustments were made to sights and first we fired from the prone position lying on the warm, sandy soil, then kneeling and finally standing where my accuracy diminished as my 6'6" frame swayed in the breeze. To finish we did fast firing with reloading while the targets were raised and lowered in five second intervals. All the time we were gaining confidence in our ability to handle a high velocity rifle. Next it was our turn to work the targets while the other column - all twenty of them - fired. It had been a full and interesting day so I had a lot to take in and mull over in my mind as I squatted in the butts, the rifle shots passing harmlessly overhead sounding like whip cracks.

CHAPTER 3

New Years Gift

My first call-up papers arrived a month after the training day. I was required to undertake a sixteen day tour of duty and I felt a sense of relief that, at last, things were moving.

A cold winter morning found me back at Morris Depot where I joined the khaki clad throngs milling around the main hall. To start with we had to divide up into sticks of four. Old hands joined friends from previous call-ups but I quickly found two obvious newcomers in their crisp new uniforms and we soon coaxed another stray into our midst. We introduced ourselves. Gordon, the tallest of the three had experienced one previous call-up but Ian and Sam were rookies like myself.

The first two days consisted of refresher courses and a round of lectures, similar to my first training day. On the third day we drew our rifles, ammunition and equipment from the armoury. Only then were we informed as to the area we would proceed to for the next two weeks. We would be divided into sections going to the Honde Valley, Umtali, Chipinga and Beit Bridge. Our stick was designated, with the vast majority to Chipinga, a village in the notorious Eastern Border area. From there we would be divided up and sent out to guard farms, tea and coffee estates and any vulnerable installations such as bridges, electricity stations, dams, etc.

It was an area that had seen increased activity in the preceding months, with incursions by ZANLA terrorists and border clashes with the Frelimo forces in Mozambique. Only a few weeks earlier, a farmer had been killed and his family seriously injured when their Peugeot station wagon had been blown up by a land mine.

At three o'clock the next morning, with the temperature near zero, we left the darkened police camp in a convoy of lorries. These consisted of Isuzu and Nissan open backed 10 tonners with water filled tyres and sandbagged bodywork as a tentative protection against land mines. We huddled on the dubious comfort of the sandbags, while the night air rushed by, blinking the tears from our eyes, not from fear, but from the cold. The only break in the dark landscape rushing past was the occasional pin prick of light from the glowing embers of a dying fire within a cluster of African huts, the orangey red glow streaking past as we sped by, the occupants sleeping in comparative comfort.

Some two hours of numbness had passed before the first streak of daylight on the horizon heralded the coming of the dawn. If anything it seemed to get even colder as the fingers of light crept towards us.

It was fully light when, to our relief, the convoy stopped for a much needed break. Within seconds of scrambling off the trucks, there was the incongruous sight of about a hundred or more men standing in a line, for about a quarter of a mile, at what must have qualified as the world's longest toilet. Our fingers were so numb that we impatiently struggled to undo our fly buttons and it was not until the sun rose into the sky, to warm us, that most of us could make ourselves respectable again.

We carried on to the Police Camp in Rusape where a welcoming cup of tea and hot breakfast greeted us. It was as we clambered back up onto the trucks that I heard a nearby call. "Rod, what the hell are you doing here?"

I turned to see Skalk Van de Merwe, a colleague of mine, about to climb into the driver's seat.

"I didn't realise that you were driving us," I returned.

"Better than sitting in the back," he retorted. "You must join us, the transport section is great."

There was no more time for conversation but, as I tried to make myself comfortable on the sandbags, I decided to find out more about the transport section. Skalk had given me food for thought.

Fortunately, the sun was well up by now and the day was warming up fast. From now on the road twisted and turned to climb towards the mountains that surround Umtali. Soon we bade farewell to the Honde Valley contingent at the Inyanga turn off. They had our heartfelt good wishes because Honde Valley had an unenviable reputation for land mines plus much terrorist activity. At least we were travelling on tarmac roads all the way to Chipinga.

As we ascended Christmas Pass the black diesel smoke pumped out of the exhaust as we laboured up the hill and, with much grating of gears, we broached the lip of the valley at a walking pace. The picturesque border town of Umtali sprawled in the valley below, shimmering in the heat haze, with the sun glinting off corrugated iron roofs and windows. A range of great granite and tree lined mountains ringed the bowl shaped valley like sentinels. Memories of many a happy holiday flooded back but now I felt slightly awkward and out of place, arriving on a police truck wearing a combat uniform. We turned into an unfamiliar road and through the gates of the police camp, eventually debussing near a large marquee. A police inspector came hurrying up and, after a brief resume of the local war situation, we retired to the marquee to partake of another hearty breakfast of sizzling hot bacon, eggs and sausage, served on a tin plate, all washed down with a steaming mug of strong coffee. Then we were off on the last leg of our journey.

From now on we were in the war zone and for the first time we sat with rifles cocked and at the ready, no talking and fully alert. Civilians travelling along these roads were protected by a military convoy system, set up because of the risk of ambush. We passed the first convoy, forming up on the outskirts of the town, and then we sped along the now deserted road. Slowly the terrain changed from woodland to sandy thorn bush and scrub. We were heading south now, with the craggy mountain ranges guarding the eastern border always on the horizon. Occasionally a distinctive Baobab tree would appear, looking like a child's drawing of a tree, the wide trunk and distorted branches out of proportion, looking almost as though they are planted upside down with the roots in the air.

The sun was high in the sky when we reached Birchenough Bridge, the largest single span bridge in Africa, and, when it was completed

in 1935, the third longest single-arch suspension bridge in the world. Its resemblance to the Sidney Harbour Bridge is no coincidence as the designer, Ralph Freeman, was also the structural designer of the famous bridge in Australia. The silver steel structure glittered beneath the deep blue African sky, a monument to man's engineering ability rising from the sandbanks of the Sabi river, contrasting incongruously with the mud huts and rickety store buildings lining the approach road, outside of which hawkers stood hopefully offering bananas, groundnuts and other wares. Across the river the red, corrugated iron roof of the hotel beckoned us, but there was to be no refreshing iced drink as there had been on my previous visits, when holidaying in the Eastern Districts.

We had only enough time to change the guard on the bridge. The deeply tanned veterans cheerfully leaving their sandbagged bunker for the comforts of home. We then turned towards the mountains that we had shadowed for so many miles. In a matter of minutes we had left the heat of the Sabi valley and were met by a cooler mountain breeze. Gone were the thorn scrub and baobabs, now there was bush grass, msasa and eucalyptus trees. Higher and higher we climbed until we were close to the green slopes and craggy walls of the surrounding mountains. At last we had reached our destination.

Chipinga, like most small Rhodesian towns, was no more than a sleepy village with a dusty main street, the inevitable colonial style hotel bordered by a deep veranda or stoep, was in the centre, with a post office, garage and general store. Finally, we lumbered through to the police camp, where we were met by the cheers of the men we had come to relieve.

As we lined up to hear of our allotted task, Ian was moved to another group so it was just Sam, Gordon and myself who accompanied Pat, the resident engineer, back to New Years Gift tea estate. The estate lay in a small fertile valley, ringed by high tree covered hills, close to the main road that we had so recently travelled along. We had heard horrific tales of the dangers from land mines in this area but Pat had no qualms as he swung onto the dirt road and sped towards the office buildings. We soon learnt that the locals showed no fear of their situation, risking land mines, ambushes and attacks daily. We townies were the jittery ones.

Our task for the next two weeks was to protect the managers, engineers, their families and their homes. Unfortunately, when the estate was first carved out of the bush, many years ago, a war situation would have been furthest from the minds of the developers. Consequently, the houses were scattered over a wide area and were some distance from the factory buildings and offices. Our accommodation was a cottage in the largest fenced enclosure, which included the general manager and engineer's house. Pat's house was separate within its own security fence and there were two other houses, temporarily unoccupied. All enclosures had lockable steel gates that were shut at sunset and reopened at sunrise. We were given custody of the keys and, as by now the light was fading, we locked up and settled down to our first nights duty. We contemplated keeping a guard all night but, as we were all dog - tired from the trip, we soon threw caution to the wind and slept right through until dawn.

Right from the start Gordon insisted on doing all the cooking, which Sam and I thought was uncommonly decent of him. We should have known there was a catch to it and, as the days slowly passed by, we gradually became more bored and restless at the enforced inactivity. We had nothing to do except talk, play cards or go for a short walk, whilst Gordon happily occupied his time fussing around the kitchen, playing housewife. This earned him the nickname Mary to which, fortunately, he took no offence. The only break to our monotony was a telephone call to our wives once a day, as we were fortunate in having the use of a phone in the house.

New Years Gift was one of three company estates in the area and there was a powerful radio link between them. The aerial was sited on a steep hill at the head of the valley and, on Friday, Pat asked us to join him to replace the batteries, as the radio signal was becoming distorted. We readily agreed and went with him in his Land Rover to the base of the hill. We started the steep climb and I felt sorry for the two labourers, each carrying an enormous lead acid battery on their shoulders, but my sympathy was unfounded as, within a hundred yards, they had disappeared onwards and upwards into the trees and rocks above us. We were left gasping and Gordon soon called it a day, sinking down thankfully under the shade of an overhanging rock. With grim determination I pushed on and, with lungs bursting and legs aching, I eventually made it to the top, with Sam not far behind. Meanwhile, the maintenance party had already changed the batteries and were ready for the descent.

"Do us a favour," I gasped, collapsing onto a convenient rock. "Give us five minutes."

As I regained my breath I took in my surroundings. The view was magnificent, with New Years Gift tea estate away to my left, the dark green tea bushes, in uniform rows, laid out in military precision. Beyond, the hills gave way to the grey haze of the Sabi valley shimmering in the heat. To my right the hills stretched up to the rocky outcrops of the mountains marking the Mozambique border. The peace and tranquillity was absolute. The only sound that filtered up from below was that of a donkey braying near a cluster of huts. As I rose to leave I was on eye level with a hawk, wings motionless as it rode a thermal. I was reluctant to leave. The climb up had been hard, but the reward was ample compensation, but it was time to go down again, and this would be easy, or so I thought. As we started down the steep slope, my calf muscles had to work in an unnatural way as I battled to stop myself sliding down out of control. My toes were forced into the caps of my leather boots and, by the time I hobbled to the Land Rover, my feet were raw with blisters. Our role as guards to the maintenance party had been totally misplaced.

CHAPTER 4

Attack

It became obvious by now that we had not received any formal training as to how exactly to guard an area so spread out as a tea estate. We had just been sent there and told what our overall duty was, but by Saturday we had finally decided on a plan of action, should we come under attack. The daylight hours were guaranteed almost one hundred percent safe. The twilight and night hours held the most potential danger. We decided, rightly or wrongly, not to keep up a watch all night. Our arrangement was that the area to patrol was too large and the undergrowth around the circumference of the compound too thick to be able to see anything even in the brightest moonlight. We decided, therefore, that we would take it in turns to be last to turn in during the early hours of the morning. Our cottage faced the main gate at a corner of the compound. In the event of any action, Sam would fire from the bedroom, which faced a thick wood from where an attack was possible. Gordon would fire from the veranda, which faced directly onto the gateway, while I would fire from the lounge, which faced onto the tea plantation itself. Although there were sandbagged trenches outside we were so naive that we felt that we would be safer inside the building. We decided that an outside light would be left on, as it partly illuminated the main gate and we hoped it would deter any aggressors from coming too close.

The estate manager, a member of the local police reserve could cover the rear of the compound from his house and for the next few days the other houses would be unoccupied because personnel were away on leave and Pat had decided to take a weekend break in Salisbury.

The evening after our mountaineering escapade, we sat playing cards until eleven when Sam and Gordon retired to bed. Sam slept in full kit, even keeping his boots on. Gordon, on the other hand, always changed into silk pyjamas which would have been more in keeping with a long cigarette holder than the FN rifle he carried at all times.

It was my turn to be last up so I had a bath and then read for a while. At midnight I turned off the inside lights and lay down. I must have started to doze when a sound suddenly jerked me on full alert. I had heard a metallic echo as if a fence post had been struck. Rolling over, I shook Sam violently. As I tried to rouse him, my words were drowned by a cacophony of sound. The ground shook from explosions with, above it all, a rattle like pebbles rolling down a corrugated iron roof.

I made to draw back the curtains and open a window but then thought that that was a bit formal, when someone was obviously trying to kill us, so with no more ado, I let rip a full magazine of twenty rounds through the window. The sound of shattering glass was drowned by the deafening explosions of the rifle firing in the small room. By now Sam was by my side and I could hear Gordon firing from the veranda. I suddenly went cold with fear because the outside light not only allowed us to see the main gate, but ironically it also lit up the house and made it an easier target for the enemy. I cursed our stupidity and, although the switch was outside the back door, I plucked up courage, burst outside, flicked the switch off and leapt back into the relative protection of the kitchen. Crawling into the lounge I recommenced firing but after a few rounds my rifle jammed. With sweating hands and furrowed brow I frantically muttered the training procedure to myself. "Remove magazine, clear rifle and reload, cock and fire," I did this, but after firing only one round, the rifle jammed again.

"Fool," I cursed myself. "Step up the gas pressure."

The din outside ceased as suddenly as it had started. I sat in the dark panting slightly, the adrenaline coursing through my veins. The quiet seemed ominous and my nerves were shattered by the sudden ringing of the telephone near me.

"Hello?" I enquired. There didn't seem anything more appropriate to say under the circumstances. It was the estate manager enquiring after our health.

"We're OK," I assured him.

"I've contacted the Chipinga police on the agric alert so we should be getting some help soon," he informed me.

I sank back with relief, all was quiet and all we had to do was wait. Suddenly, there was an exclamation from Gordon. "Bloody hell, look at my groundsheet."

I crawled through to the veranda, bumping into Sam on the way. In the excitement Gordon, like me, had thrown caution to the wind and sprayed bullets through the windows, completely forgetting his police issue groundsheet was hanging from the French windows as a temporary curtain. We gazed up at the window where the moon and stars could be seen glistening through numerous bullet holes in Gordon's shredded groundsheet. In our nervous state we all just collapsed with laughter, the thought of Gordon in his silk pyjamas firing a rifle in anger through his groundsheet was just too much and the three of us just rolled around the floor in uncontrollable mirth.

After what seemed hours, we became conscious of a low hum in the distance, which steadily increased to the drone of a bumble bee. It was an aircraft slowly approaching and, after what seemed an age, a flare was dropped, bathing the now silent tea plantation in an unnatural ghostly light. Peering from the windows we had neither sight nor sound of our attackers and, so far as we could see, the perimeter fence was still intact.

As we watched, a beam of light flashed on the steel mesh gate and the sound of a vehicle could be heard slowly approaching. We left the confines of the cottage to meet the two army trucks that loomed out of the half light. We were immediately surrounded by soldiers demanding to know details of the raid.

"Right, lets spread out in case they reform and counter attack," ordered a lieutenant, who appeared to be in charge.

"You," pointing at me. "Come and show us the way through to the other side of the compound."

"It would be safer if we telephoned through to the estate manager first," I pointed out. "Otherwise he's liable to shoot at anything that moves."

This was duly done and then we moved through the grounds to meet the manager on the steps of his house. The lieutenant decided to put men in defensive positions throughout the perimeter of the compound and I went with him and a small group, until we came across some dug out foundations near some out buildings.

"This will do," whispered the officer. "Spread out and lie down in this trench."

The soldiers were carrying full kit with them and soon had sleeping bags and blankets spread out. I tried making myself comfortable at one end of the trench but, as I had left the house in a hurry, all I had was what I stood up in, a jersey, combat jacket, trousers and shoes. Not only was the ground hard and stony but, being the middle of winter, the temperature was nippy to say the least. I mentioned my plight to the lieutenant who reluctantly lent me a blanket. Soon we had all bedded down, as best we could, and at first, just reflecting on the nights events and the excitement caused me to glow with warmth from the adrenaline surge but, as the night slowly passed by I grew steadily colder, until I was screwed up into a tight ball vainly trying to preserve every ounce of warmth in my body. Sleep was out of the question and I lay listening enviously to the adjacent snoring. The hours passed with agonising slowness, the only indication of time passing was the movement of the moon, which passed ponderously across the clear, star speckled night sky.

It was with a great sense of relief that I realised that the sky was lightening from the east and that, at last, the dawn was breaking. A reminder that the Mozambique border lay only a few kilometres away. The terrorists were probably well on their way back to safety by now. As the light grew stronger so tousled heads appeared from their sleeping bags, bleary eyes blinking in the light. We were soon up and heading back to the cottage where I was curious to see what damage had been done. Reaching the cottage I found Gordon and Sam drinking coffee with some young soldiers. As I greeted them I glanced at the cottage.

"How much damage did they do?" I asked.

"Nothing," grunted Sam.

"You're kidding," I replied with amazement. "It was a hell of a racket."

"Look for yourself," was Gordon's retort.

The house looked as though a bomb had hit it, shattered windows, shredded curtains, plaster chipped, but all the damage was from the inside, caused by our own shooting. Externally there wasn't a mark anywhere.

There were quite a few derisory remarks from the regular soldiers lolling about nearby regarding the Police reservists shooting at shadows.

A Land Rover soon arrived, bringing the local police and special branch detectives. I was to learn that this was a very civilised war, with every incident involving civilians and property having a proper police investigation, as well as a follow-up as far as possible to trace the instigators.

Expecting to be questioned about the attack, we were surprised and annoyed when not only were we ignored but once again the insults were bandied about regarding Police reservists in general and townies in particular. It was beginning to look as though we had never come under attack at all and the powers that be felt that we had panicked and shot at nothing. In disgust we decided to go for a walk and, with morale low, we wandered off around the rear of the compound. Baffled by the lack of damage we still could not understand what we had heard, the explosions and rattling on the corrugated iron roof were very real, we could not have imagined it.

As we approached the lane near one of the unoccupied houses we spotted strange marks on the ground. A blast of some sort had blown the dust away, exposing the hard earth beneath. Walking on towards the house we noticed something strange about the roof and windows.

On closer inspection it was evident that a heavy explosion had holed the rear wall, lifting the eaves and blowing the windows out. The room inside was a shambles, with the walls pockmarked by shrapnel, furniture broken and ornaments strewn around.

"Look," called Sam. "There's a hole in the fence."

It was quite evident that some form of rocket had been fired at the house from outside the fence. As we hurried back to report our find, a group of soldiers ran in from the opposite direction.

"The house over there has been mortared," they reported.

Now the tables had turned, we were vindicated and derision was replaced by friendly banter.

"You buggers must have shat yourselves."

"It must have been a hell of a racket."

It eventually turned out that one house had been badly damaged by a number of mortar shells and the house next door had mortar craters in the garden, but somehow had sustained no damage. The house we had spotted had had two direct hits from RPG rockets, and, on closer inspection, our own cottage had a line of bullet holes raked across the chimney and a branch had been ripped from a large overhanging tree, possibly by a rocket. Numerous spent cartridge cases were found that had been fired from AK47 automatic rifles and RPD machine guns. It was the heaviest attack up to that time and we felt fully vindicated when, a few days later, we read a report in the Rhodesia Herald national newspaper that credited us with having repelled the attackers.

Whilst the army awaited transport back to their base camp, one of the squaddies cleared up our mystery noise.

"That wasn't anything rattling on your roof," he said. "That was the sound of automatic fire from an AK heard from the wrong end of the barrel."

We were really surprised that the army wasn't going to carry out an immediate follow up operation, even though our view from the summit of the aerial hill made it obvious which route the terrorists would have taken. Unfortunately our views on the subject were regarded as not being of much help to the professionals. Therefore, imagine our annoyance when, a few days later, a full scale search was instigated, with troops being housed on the estate and air lifted by an Alouette helicopter into exactly the area we had described, albeit too late to be of any use. The terrorists would have been safely back in Mozambique by then.

Over the next few days life returned to the boredom that we had endured, before the brief excitement of the attack. It was with a sense of relief therefore when Roy, the estate manager, called round to see if one of us would escort him to a small plantation just off the Melsetter road, where macadamia nuts were being grown. Sam and Gordon weren't interested but I leapt at the chance to get out of the tea estate, albeit for just an afternoon. I enjoyed the change of scenery, as the Land Rover sped past mountains and valleys, glad to be free from the confines of the tea estate. We turned off onto a dirt side road and quickly accelerated into a valley, with the gay abandon that I had come to expect from the locals. My grip tightened around my rifle as we sped past rocks and bushes - ideal ambush sites - and we slowed to turn up a narrow track, just short of a huge crater in the gravel.

"That's where the family hit the landmine in their Peugeot the other day," Roy mentioned nonchalantly.

I now wished that I hadn't been so eager to ride shot gun, particularly as Roy continued to hurl the Land Rover at breakneck speed up the rough track. The undergrowth thickened until we suddenly burst into a clearing, where African labourers were tending rows of young plants. As we were within sight of the Mozambique border I was glad when Roy had concluded his business and even happier when we regained the relative safety of the main tarred road.

The remaining few days dragged slowly by, the only excitement being when the generator packed up one night, plunging us into darkness, but this time we were a bit more professional, immediately diving for the trenches and keeping watch until dawn. The cause, we found out the next day, was just mechanical failure which was quickly rectified.

At last the day arrived when we were to leave and we waited impatiently for the relief troops to arrive. We boarded the trucks for the return trip home and I was really looking forward to sleeping in my own bed but we were fated not to get home that night. As we approached Nyonyodzi, near the Hot Springs holiday resort one of the trucks slowed and stopped with brake trouble. Temporary repairs were made but too much time had passed and it was twilight before we arrived at the Umtali police camp and were told that an overnight stop was necessary. We were issued with camp beds, otherwise called stretchers, and ushered into a large marquee for the night, but it wasn't long before the pub was sniffed out and a large proportion of our contingent then made up for lost time and for their two weeks abstinence.

It was well after midnight before the last dark figure lurched into the marquee, stumbling over the other occupants. When at last all was quiet the process started again, but in reverse, as the call of nature enticed them outside again. It wasn't until the small hours of the morning that I eventually drifted off to sleep, only to be woken by a lone snorer. With over a hundred inmates, we had to have one champion snorer. After a few timid attempts to silence him, someone's patience snapped and he was shaken violently. Thinking he was being assaulted, the slumberer retaliated viciously with his fists. Eventually they were parted and explanations given. Quiet descended again, but there was no way that I would be able to sleep, so my thoughts went back over the past two weeks.

It was quite apparent that we had been hopelessly and inadequately trained for the task given us. We had been given no instruction on what to do when coming under attack. With mortars and rockets flying around we should never have stayed in the house. It would have been safer to have run to the trenches with their sandbagged protection. We had had no instruction on using the agric-alert system that all farmhouses and estates had installed in these dangerous times. On reflection it was also obvious that we were only there as a token, armed presence, which was not going to deter the action of a determined terrorist. I decided that the prospect of innumerable call-ups with such boredom and tension was not for me and that, as soon as I got back, I would investigate the possibilities of transferring into the transport section.

CHAPTER 5

Convoys

"Come on then," she commanded. "Which vehicle is yours?"

I pointed to the Bedford supplied by the driving school. I wasn't sure, from her diminutive size, whether she could even reach the door handle but, by the way she pulled herself up into the cab, the slightly built lady was obviously well used to heavy vehicles.

I had wasted no time, after my first call-up, in having some driving lessons to obtain the heavy vehicle licence necessary to gain a transfer to the transport section. Now it was time for my driving test and the tester was a petite grey haired old lady, who looked like someone's favourite grandmother rather than the archetypal trucker.

"Come on Mister Wells," she snapped. "I haven't got all day."

I pulled myself together and carefully drove the set route, as instructed, finishing with a reverse test. Finally, she looked at me with a smile.

"OK, you've passed, just one thing though - you drive too slowly!"

Whilst completing the official pass form, she went on to relate her own experiences, driving heavy vehicles during the Second World War in the WAAC's.

I now had to take a Police test and, a week later, I was seated next to a heavy set, dour policeman in a military Bedford R.M. The brakes were extremely sharp and, on the first application, I shot the tester into the windscreen, his clipboard and notes tumbling to the floor.

"You haven't had much experience of driving heavy vehicles, have you?" He asked with heavy sarcasm.

Once again I performed all the required manoeuvres asked of me. When the test ended, he checked his notes and then conceded that I had passed.

"Just one thing though, you drive too fast!"

I had quickly adjusted back to civilian life after my sojourn at the 'sharp end'. The war had not reached Salisbury yet and the routine eight to five existence carried on, with socialising at the weekend consisting of braivleis (barbecues), swimming and entertaining. I was also busy finishing off a complete restoration of an Austin Healey sports car that I had owned for a number of years. The excitement of the attack at New Years Gift had started to fade when, in October, my next set of call up papers arrived requiring me to report for duty in the last two weeks of November. I had already applied for a transfer to the transport section and hoped that this would be my last regular call up.

I duly reported back at the Morris Depot and, once again, we had a round of lectures, followed by a kit issue and the inevitable trip to the firing range.

"The area you are going to has had a lot of landmine incidents." was our bleak introduction at the firing range.

November is generally the start of the summer and the rainy season in Rhodesia so the weather was hot and sweltering. We stood in the shade whenever possible, with the temperature hovering around 35oC. In the heat, the drone of the instructor's voice made it difficult to concentrate. It was rumoured that we were heading south this time, to carry out convoy duties in the low veldt, between Fort Victoria and Beit Bridge. The convoys had been started after a group of South African motor cyclists had been held up and killed near Nuanetsi, some few months previously. Until that incident the main terrorist activity had been concentrated in the North and East, unfortunately, the problem had now spread South.

"………three volunteers. You three will do."

I jerked out of my daydream and back to the present to see the lecturer's finger pointing in my direction.

"Pay attention!" he snapped.

"Over there," he indicated a sandy track adjacent to us. "I've laid two dud landmines."

"When searching for mines you prod with one of these."

He then took a steel rod, approximately a metre long, and proceeded to demonstrate in the sandy ground before him.

"Work in a line, prodding about three inches apart. If the probe pushes easily into soft earth it means that the soil has recently been disturbed. You then lie down and slowly scoop the dirt away, being cautious of booby traps, until you locate the mine - right, you three start moving forward in a line abreast."

Slowly we moved forward, probing all the time. The ground had been compacted hard by the numerous vehicles passing over it. Suddenly my probe pushed easily into the earth.

"I've found something Sir," I informed the instructor.

"Carry on and feel for the mine then," came back the reply.

As I lay down on the baked earth, the heat swamped me as though I was on top of an oven.

"Before you start, let me just warn you that I've laid a booby trap with a small charge attached. If you probe carefully, you've nothing to worry about. Having said that, it won't hurt you, it will just blow dust into your eyes."

Was he fooling, I thought incredulously? Surely even a small charge would blow my fingers off? Cursing my luck I reluctantly started scraping the soft soil away. The task was made harder by the sweat dribbling into my eyes, not just from the heat, but also from fear, from the uncertainty of whether the instructor was kidding or not. All of a sudden, this seemed like the real thing.

As I continued scraping away I became conscious of the circle of onlookers slowly moving away, some wisely seeking the slender protection of the spindly msasa tree trunks.

"He must be getting close," someone wisecracked. "Look, even the instructor has moved away now."

Trying hard to stop my hand shaking, and with the sweat forming rivulets on the ground, I suddenly touched hard metal and the khaki camouflaged edge of the land mine was revealed in the sandy hollow.

"I've found it," I gasped.

"OK, up you get," came the welcome response.

I got up with relief, there was no booby trap after all, it was just his little joke, my legs felt wobbly and I was feeling slightly dizzy. The lesson was completed and then we thankfully filed over to the firing range.

Our last task was to set the sights on our rifles. I was dying for a drink and was still feeling slightly groggy from the tension of the landmine and the heat. I knew that there was a water tap in the butts but, as luck would have it, I had to line up to fire first.

"We're running a bit behind time, so as soon as your sights are OK move into the butts to relieve the lads there. Then they can come back and set their rifles."

With salvation in sight I forced myself to concentrate and shot like someone possessed. After just one adjustment I was relieved to hear the result crackle through the radio.

"Ten inners."

I made my way into the butts thankfully. Never has a drink of water tasted so fine. I was lucky because, before the day was out, we had two casualties sent to hospital suffering from heat exhaustion.

We left Salisbury, this time in the pampered luxury of air conditioned Mercedes Benz coaches. I lay back in the reclining seat, my mind running over the letter I had received the day before leaving, with the official confirmation of my transfer to the transport section. This should be my last regular call-up and my thoughts ran over the problems facing my family and business. I would still have a military commitment but at least I wouldn't be way from work for any more lengthy periods. Perhaps we could carry on but the future was very uncertain.

"Look out driver!" the frantic cry woke me from my daydream.

At one hundred kilometres an hour we were almost upon a herd of cows blocking the road. The driver, who appeared to have dozed off, jerked back to life and, with a screech of tyres, we were all flung forward and stopped within inches of the baleful stare of the long horn cattle, unaware of the disaster that had nearly befallen them.

"Whew, I thought we were goners then," my neighbour sighed with relief. "It would be ironic to be croaked in a motor accident when there's a war on."

Our destination was Fort Victoria, the first settlement of the pioneers in 1890. The wide, tree-lined streets and the remaining two towers of the old fort, still exuded some of the pioneering spirit that had helped create this modern country from virgin bush. The curfew bell still rang traditionally at 9 p.m. each evening.

We were billeted in the local theatre and, with the majority seeking out the nearest pub, we had a repeat of our last night in Umtali with many bloodshot eyes on parade the next morning.

Still uncertain as to our actual deployment, I and about two dozen others were separated from the main body and led through to a briefing room, where it was confirmed that we were indeed on convoy duty.

There were four convoys operating in the southern area at that time, with the main ones – codenamed 'blue and 'yellow' - on the well used route between Fort Victoria and Beit Bridge, on the border with South Africa. Another convoy branched of at Ngundu Halt to wind its way to Chiredzi, in Hippo Valley. The last convoy went between Fort Victoria and Birchenough Bridge near the Eastern Highlands. In addition there were ranging patrols, codenamed 'green', that patrolled specific sectors ahead of the convoys. All convoy vehicles were equipped with two-way radios and the main radio relay stations were at Fort Victoria, Rutenga and Beit Bridge. As the convoys entered or left each sector, so the relevant radio station had to be informed. We were given a list of the appropriate call signs, which once again showed up our inadequate training because a few of us had missed out on radio procedure.

I was selected for the first route and, at last, we were divided off, four persons per vehicle. Twelve of us with three vehicles were allotted the 'blue' convoy, based at Beit Bridge, and we made our way outside to await the arrival of our vehicles. It was nearly eleven o'clock and a variety of trucks, Land Rovers and mine protected vehicles were trickling in, depositing weary Police reservists ready for their return trip to the 'bright lights', as the cities were known.

A Bedford RL, with returning troops, swung in close to us and I heard a shout. Looking up I was surprised to see Sam, one of my companions from New Years Gift. Although he smiled in greeting, he looked tired and dishevelled.

"Christ, this is a hot area," he imparted as he swung down from the back of the truck.

"What job have they given you?" he enquired.

"Beit Bridge convoy," I replied.

"Your bloody lucky, we went to a base camp in the middle of nowhere and got ambushed going in, before the tour even started."

"Was anyone hurt?" I asked with interest.

"No, we were lucky, there was an armed escort with us, but even then we had to wait ages for relief."

There was no more time to find out more and I bade him farewell as, at that moment, our vehicles arrived. They were Mazda B1800 ½ ton pickups with a Browning machine gun mounted on a pedestal in the rear. We loaded up our kit and made our way down to the troops canteen for a quick snack, before lining up for our first run to Beit Bridge.

Almost every town and village had a troops canteen, run voluntarily by such organisations as the Women's Institute and Rotary. They provided good, basic nourishment at low prices and were a godsend when travelling at odd hours of day and night.

Over lunch we introduced ourselves and Mike, who with one or two others, was from the Midlands town of Gwelo and an ex-regular policeman, volunteered to lead the first convoy. We set off to the road block where the convoys assembled before the departure time of twelve noon. Slowly, the column started to lengthen with cars, pickups and the odd motorbike, many of the cars filled with families off on holiday to South Africa. Five minutes before the off, the drivers were briefed on the speed at which we would travel and the distance to maintain between vehicles and, most important of all, what to do if the convoy was attacked.

If the road wasn't blocked, everyone was to drive as fast as possible through the ambush zone, but if the road was blocked, they were told to stop and leave the vehicle for the comparative safety of a ditch or whatever cover was available.

At last it was time to move off and, like the wagon trains of the wild west, we slowly set off in single file, the speed gradually building up to about ninety kilometres an hour. Our three protection vehicles were situated at the head, middle and rear of the convoy.

Soon we were winding our way down the curves of Providential Pass, the modern engineered tarmac road making a mockery of the term 'Pass' where, eighty five years previously, the scout and hunter, Courtney Selous had guided the pioneer column through the hills.

As we approached Ngundu Halt so the countryside became more undulating until we reached the junction with the Chiredzi road, where a number of vehicles left us to join the convoy into the Hippo Valley.

The granite kopjes and high ngomos closed in menacingly as the road twisted and turned amongst them, the gunners swivelling the machine guns from side to side, fully alert to the risk of ambush. Soon we rounded the last curve and hurried across the bridge spanning the Lundi river, a sign pointing up the old strip road to where the Rhino Hotel lay hidden amongst the great granite boulders. The hotel was now closed and was used only by the security forces as a base camp, from which one of the 'green' patrols operated.

Memories stirred of more peaceful days, before the comparatively new wide tarmac road by-passed the hotel, when hippos would sometimes wander past the buildings at night, of travellers stranded between the flood waters of the Lundi and Nuanetsi rivers, with the unheard of possibility of the pub running dry.

Heading away from the granite kopjes and into the mopane woodlands of the low veldt, the heat noticeably increased along with the constant singing of cicadas. Over to our right, I caught sight of a couple of impala antelopes watching us impassively from the shade of the trees as we sped by.

As we approached Rutenga, our radio call sign changed and the sound of the approaching northbound 'yellow' convoy became audible. The signal gradually strengthened until suddenly, like two trains passing, the vehicles clattered past with here a fleeting glimpse of a face, there a hand waving, the glint of machine guns, and then calm. Without slackening pace, we sped on past Nuanetsi and onward to our only halt for refreshment at the Lion and Elephant hotel, situated on the sandy banks of the dried up Bubye River.

Gratefully, we parked in the shade of the over hanging trees and gulped down large glasses of iced orange juice, acquired from the bar. We gazed across the parched expanse of the dry river bed as it waited for the first flash flood of the rainy season.

The break was over all too quickly and once more we headed south, the convoy snaking along the remaining 70 kilometres before arriving at Beit Bridge, which was to be our home for the next two weeks.

We reported to the police station, refuelled the trucks ready for an early start the next morning and then followed the directions we had been given to reach the camp, set idyllically on the banks of the Limpopo river overlooking the impressive grey, steel, lattice work of Beit Bridge itself. The bridge carried both road and rail as a tenuous but incredibly important link with South Africa. The great grey-green, greasy Limpopo River of Rudyard Kipling's Just-So story looked rather sparkling and refreshing.

Our camp consisted of a number of low wooden buildings, one of which incorporated the kitchen and mess, another the toilet block and radio room. The third was our sleeping quarters, laid out like a barrack room with rows of beds down either side with no pretence of comfort or privacy.

That evening we got to know each other a little better and it was decided that as Mike was an ex-regular policeman he would be our section leader for the duration. We also decided that, although four of us were allotted to each vehicle, we could easily carry out our duties with just three, which would enable us to operate a rota whereby each of us could take one day off in three. We would also take it in turns to be lead vehicle, centre or tail end Charlie. This was one advantage of the somewhat lack of instruction and training - we could make our own 'game plans' up to a certain extent.

After supper Inspector Gowan made himself known to us. As he was the Member in Charge at the local Police station we came under his jurisdiction. Every evening he would give us the situation report (sitrep) which noted all terrorist incidents and sightings close to the main road that might affect us.

We retired early as we would have a dawn start, with the convoy departing at 7.00 am. We slept fitfully, however, because the rumbling trains, bringing the country's vital petrol supplies, echoed across the steel bridge at regular intervals throughout the night.

The next morning the air was cool, clear and refreshing but, with the previous day's temperature at 45°C, we knew that this pleasantness would be short lived. I took the first stint on the machine gun, the slip stream pushing me back into the safety harness. I wore a crash helmet and visor, although the helmet would have been of more use in an accident than of stopping a bullet.

A few kilometres out of Beit Bridge, my sight was attracted by some warthogs running away from the roadside, tails erect in alarm. As this was a good area for seeing wild animals the boredom of the trip was reduced by keeping our eyes peeled for movement, which also had the added advantage of keeping us alert for trouble. Over the next two weeks I was to spot many wild animals, normally various types of antelope, on every trip. The best siting being a giraffe and foal nibbling delicately at the nourishing young bush shoots.

When travelling as tail end Charlie, one of our tasks was to deliver mail and newspapers. A lone figure in uniform would sometimes be seen standing at the roadside, having trekked from some obscure camp, his only contact with civilisation being a bundle of papers hurled from our passing vehicle. A regular problem we had to contend with was when a vehicle in the convoy broke down, either with a minor ailment such as a puncture, or with a more serious mechanical failure. It never ceased to amaze me, the number of cars that would start the long trek through hostile country with no preparation. Worn tyres, broken fan belts, cracked hoses, worn out ignition points and spark plugs were but a few of the more common causes of failure.

When a breakdown did occur, the driver would be relieved to think that he had some willing helpers to sort out his problem, only to watch in dismay as we melted away into the surrounding bush to throw a 360° protective ring around his vehicle, whilst he sweated away in the heat. If the breakdown was too serious, a 'Green' patrol vehicle would be called up for assistance and they would tow the offending vehicle to the nearest point of safety or, if close enough, to Beit Bridge itself.

After our arrival on the first day we had eagerly crowded into the ablution block for a refreshing cool shower but, to our consternation, the cold tap only belched forth hot water. The reason was that the weather was so hot, at 46°C in the shade, that our cold water supply, which was fed from a large galvanised iron tank suspended above the shower room, was heated by the blazing sun all day. Therefore, the tank acted as a boiler, which meant that a cool shower was impossible. Being exposed to the elements on the back of the trucks, our already tanned skin burnt to a deep reddish brown, even my finger nails became yellowy-brown as if nicotine stained.

November was the beginning of our rainy season and, on the third day, we were cooled by refreshing showers and from then on the temperature cooled to the high thirties Celsius.

Although pleasantly situated on the banks of the Limpopo, our camp was within two hundred metres of a sewage farm. If the breeze was in the wrong direction we would awake, not only to an unpleasant smell, but to a burning sensation in nose and throat. Fortunately this happened only rarely.

The bridge itself was protected by the South African army. The electricity supply for Beit Bridge was supplied from Messina, a small town a few kilometres across the border. We weren't too impressed on the few occasions when the lights flickered out and we were all put on maximum alert in case of sabotage, especially after a long day on the convoy.

The South African border guards would quite often stroll over to our camp for a chat and a drink. Late one afternoon we were invited over to their quarters, so we strolled along the riverbank and clambered up the huge iron structure to the roadway above.

"Come this way, it's more interesting," beckoned our guide.

An iron ladder led down to a narrow cat-walk suspended beneath the railway line. Not having a very good head for heights, I found the sight of the brown water, lazily flowing past far below the metal mesh walkway, rather disconcerting.

"Look, there's a crocodile," came a shout.

Sure enough, what at first sight, appeared to be a grey log, was slowly moving with the current. We watched it for a few moments, then as we carried on our guide stopped, listened intently and, pointing upwards, warned. "A train's coming."

The distinctive two-tone horns sounded a warning and the bridge started to tremble. As the train approached so the vibrations increased and the rumble of the iron wheels could be heard. The steam locomotive which was pulling some goods wagons snorted past overhead, the danger of bombardment by hot coals, over as quickly as it had appeared. When we finally hauled ourselves up on the other side I felt a strange sensation, to be standing on South African soil, in a military uniform, with no passport, having walked under the bridge I had driven over many times before, en route to previous holidays.

The South African quarters were an anti-climax, being no more than a sand bagged bunker with a couple of camp beds and stores. In comparison, our camp was like a five star hotel, no wonder they visited so often.

It was dark when we made our way back to the Rhodesian side, on the roadway this time but, as we walked up the riverbank to our camp, I trod warily, with thoughts of crocodiles on my mind.

On my last 'day off' I obtained a temporary visa, crossed to the South African side and hitch hiked into Messina. Christmas was only a month away and I walked into the Limpopo supermarket feeling like Aladdin on entering the cave. All around me were the sweets, crackers, toys etc. that, due to sanctions, were virtually unobtainable in Salisbury. With only a limited amount of cash left, from my two weeks allowance, I managed to procure come Callard and Bowser nougat, Quality Street chocolates and a selection of mints and Smarties for the kids. Unheard of luxuries in Rhodesia.

Soon the two week stint was over with no time for the boredom that I had suffered from on my first call-up. The last day we sped our convoy homeward, but this time we extended our break at the Lion and Elephant hotel and found a small wild life enclosure where, to our amusement, there lounged a three legged lion. It had been severely injured in the wild and, when rescued, had had to have one leg amputated but it limped agilely around its enclosure. A few weeks later we heard that it had had to be evacuated, along with all the hotel personnel, when the Bubye river burst its banks, from a sudden onslaught of rain, and the Lion and Elephant hotel was flooded out.

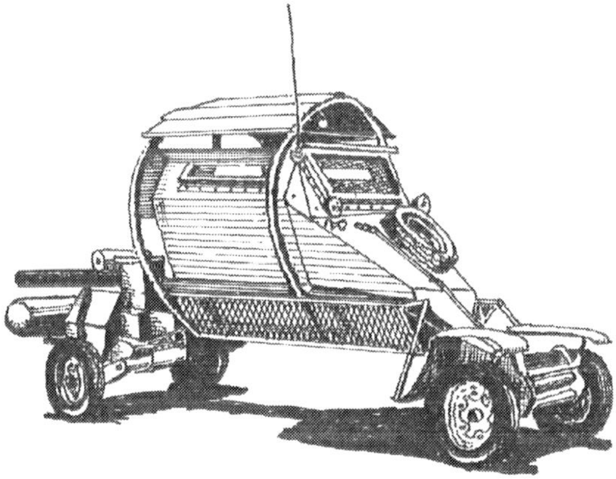

CHAPTER 6

Initiation

My first task, following the transfer to the transport unit, was to help unload some new trucks at the railway station. A few hours one evening saw this job completed and as this was officially recorded as a whole day, to be deducted from my commitment, I felt that at last things were looking up. Perhaps my business would survive these necessary interruptions after all. Little did I realise however what I had let myself in for.

"Care for a trip to Bulawayo this weekend?" enquired our commanding officer.

"Yes, certainly," I replied innocently. "What's to be done?"

"I want some Leopards delivered."

The Leopard referred to, I hasten to add, was not of the animal variety. Most landmine protected and armoured vehicles were named after animals and this particular Leopard was an armoured personnel carrier, based on Volkswagen mechanical parts. Ironically the name was a bit of a misnomer because, due to the weight of the armour plating, it was by far the slowest example of this type of vehicle, unlike its namesake.

Arriving at the depot early Saturday morning I was introduced to my companions for the weekend. John Whiteman, Mac Wemyss, Ian MacGregor and Ian St Leger. As soon as we hit the open road it became evident that it was to be a race to the finish. As luck would have it I had picked the slowest vehicle and the others were mere dots on the horizon until they vanished completely.

With a maximum speed of 100kph down hill I plodded on, first through the small town of Hartley, then Gatooma and, as there was still no sign of my compatriots, on to Que Que. As I entered the main thoroughfare, I was relieved to see four khaki coloured Leopards lined up awaiting my arrival.

After refuelling at the Police Camp, the general consensus was to stop somewhere for lunch so, a few minutes later, we drew into the car park of the Golden Mile Hotel.

After the discomfort of the steel driving seat I gratefully sank back into the upholstered opulence of the veranda chair, iced lager in hand, soothed by the sound of a small fountain trickling in the shady garden.

Soon my companions transferred from beers to shots of whiskey and time slowly drifted past, as one drink led to another, and I began to wonder if we would ever reach the transport depot in Bulawayo before it closed for the weekend.

"Relax," came the philosophical reply to my tentative enquiry. "The town will still be there when we arrive."

At last the shutters were put up around the bar and we rose from our seats to face the remainder of the trip.

With over 200 kilometres still to go and knowing that excessive drinking at midday would put me to sleep, I had ensured that my intake of booze was far lower than the other drivers. Consequently, having the slowest vehicle and the clearest head, I set off smartly to build up a slight lead and, although eventually overtaken, I was well in sight of the pack after passing through the environs of Gwelo, the next town. Ahead of us a straight, uninteresting road forged its way through the grasslands of Matabeleland for the remaining 160k.

My last sight of the others was when two Leopards crested a rise side by side in reckless abandon. I prayed that nothing was approaching them and that I wouldn't come upon the aftermath of a terrible accident.

My companions led a charmed life however, and we arrived safely although, Stopps police camp was deserted, with the transport section locked and bolted but, undeterred, we enquired at the guardhouse as to who to report to and were directed to the local police club where we eventually found the officer in charge of transport.

After the obligatory drink with the Inspector we returned to the transport compound, parked the Leopards, and were handed the keys of a large Bedford RM which would convey us back to Salisbury the next day. Concealed beneath a tarpaulin in the back were some charred and splintered remains of the rifles and kit of a PATU stick that had recently been ambushed. The story was that they had made the fatal mistake of becoming complacent, making a regular routine of visiting a river to wash. The ambush had been swift and fatal.

Soberly, we were shown to our quarters for the night, which was a dormitory with half a dozen beds lining opposite walls. After cajoling the Inspector, we managed to get the loan of a small Daihatsu police van for the evening. With the exception of St. Ledger, we had all brought civilian clothes to change into and soon we were smartened up ready to paint the town red.

Darkness was falling as we headed for the first watering hole at the Southern Sun Hotel.

"Sorry, you can't come in without a tie," said the barmaid eyeing us haughtily. "He's all right though," she continued, pointing to St. Ledger.

"But he's not wearing a tie," I protested.

"I know," she smugly replied. "But he's in army kit and we never refuse to serve anyone from the security forces."

"But we're also in the security forces," I retorted, explaining our visit from Salisbury.

"OK, I'll see what I can do," and with that she disappeared, to reappear a few moments later clutching a handful of various coloured ties.

"I've borrowed these from the waiters, you can use them if you like."

Thankfully we knotted this badge of respectability around our necks and ordered the first round of drinks. It was soon clear that my colleagues were serious drinkers, emptying their glasses as if worried that the pub might run dry. I never had been able to drink like that, so I slowed down and watched the party getting progressively merrier and merrier. After a while it was decided that a night club would be more fun and there might be some spare female company around. I had my doubts on this score but was happy to follow on. The tyres screamed in protest as we shot down the road, swerving around corners until we eventually slid to a stop outside a night club. The giggling occupants in the rear of the van collapsed against the dividing window which promptly shattered. By now I was feeling a little uneasy about the driving excesses and, visualising a night in the cells, I decided to remove the keys from MacGregor, aptly nicknamed MacGrogger, at the earliest opportunity.

We were off beer now and the hard tack was flowing like water. Mac Wymess and MacGrogger had spied two lone females who they persuaded onto the dance floor. It looked as if we were there for the remainder of the evening. That was, until two burly soldiers appeared looking for their errant girl friends. We beat a hasty retreat and, after visiting another night club, staggered back to our billet in the small hours of the morning.

We woke, blearily, and, although I had regulated my drinking, it didn't stop a sledge hammer banging my skull from the inside. We walked mope-eyed into the mess, only to be confronted by large plates of greasy egg and bacon. Mac Wyness shakily retreated.

"Anything wrong?" asked the chirpy waiter on seeing our hue turn visibly green.

As we slowly loaded our kit into the truck I realised that I was the only one in a fit state to drive. The others, looking like death warmed up, were quite happy to hand me the keys and then collapsed amongst the sandbags and promptly went to sleep.

The Bedford had seen better days and, with a maximum speed down hill of about 60 kph, slowing to under 50 kph when going uphill, the 430k journey was going to be long and arduous. The first 160k to Gwelo was uneventful but, as I turned into the main street, my attention was attracted by banging on the cab roof.

"Stop outside the Midlands Hotel," came a shout from behind.

I peered into the rear view mirror and noted that they seemed to have recovered and were looking more cheerful. Swinging into a parking place I switched off. It was 12 o'clock noon and I was feeling peckish.

I was soon to be disappointed, as we passed the dining room and headed, inevitably, for the bar. Being tired from the previous nights excesses and, as I was driving, I decided to stay 'dry' today so I just grabbed a couple of packets of crisps and returned to guard the truck and its contents.

It was nearly 1 o'clock, and the sun was making me drowsy, when my attention was caught by a down and out staggering along the street begging for money. He was obviously the worse for drink so I hoped that he would totter past me but, unfortunately, his bloodshot eyes lit up as he noticed me. His mouth twisted into a grotesque toothless smile, saliva dribbling down the stubble on his chin.

"Spare a dollar?" he leered charmingly.

"Sorry, nothing on me," I lied.

"Bull-shit," he sneered. "You guys always have money."

"I'll pay you back," he whined.

"Sorry, I haven't……"

"Come on," he interjected aggressively.

The sweat prickled down my neck as I watched him apprehensively. Would he pull a knife? Passers by hurried past with averted eyes. I wondered if he would go if I offered him my half eaten packet of crisps. He lurched closer, his breath reeking of booze and fags, when a voice spoke in my ear.

"Who's your friend?" Mac Wymess had appeared.

"He won't take no for an answer," I replied with relief at having reinforcements.

"I'll soon sort him out," was Mac's reply and, turning to the beggar he shouted. "Bugger off, voetsak you bastard."

Cowering away, the drunk stumbled off, mumbling beneath his breath. I had a twinge of sympathy but turned and thanked Mac for his help.

"That's OK, do you want a drink?" he inquired. "I'll look after the truck."

I declined his offer which, as it turned out, I was to regret, because it wasn't until 2 o'clock that they came chatting and laughing out of the pub. St. Ledger was carrying a large bottle of brandy.

"Stop at a garage and we'll get some Cokes to mix with this," he said as they clambered back up onto the truck.

The journey resumed, but I had a sneaking suspicion that the remaining 150 kilometres might turn into a pub crawl. I was due to take my wife out that evening and I didn't want to be too late.

I drove, apprehensively, into Que Que. I half suspected a shout from the back but we toured past the Sebakwe Hotel and were soon out on the open road again. Fortunately, they still had some brandy left and snatches of song occasionally drifted through my open window.

I wasn't so lucky as we arrived in Gatooma, however. At first I ignored the cries from behind and the banging on the cab roof but, eventually, I weakened and pulled into the local motel. As I squeezed the Bedford into the only vacant space, opposite the bourganvillia shrouded veranda, a cheer erupted from the back as the bar was glimpsed and at that moment a tall, overweight farmer emerged, his paunch overshadowing his dirty shorts.

"Welcome boys," he greeted us and, turning to his colleagues, obscured in the dimly lit bar, shouted. "Put 'em up bartender. The army's arrived."

It was well past closing time but, on entering the bar, it was evident that we had found the local hard core of drinkers and official drinking hours were to be ignored. The occupants heralded us as heroes, thrusting drinks into our hands. We didn't bother to enlighten them as to the real reason for our Bulawayo trip, delivering new vehicles and a non-stop binge.

As quickly as glasses were emptied so they were refilled. I regarded my almost comatose colleagues and despaired of ever getting them back to Salisbury that day. I wanted to get home, it had been a long weekend and I still had an evening out to look forward to, if we got back in time. St Ledger sank into the chair beside me.

"What's up?" he queried. "You look fed up."

I explained my predicament and, leaning towards me, he said. "You're new in transport section, so let me give you a tip. You are the driver, so you are in charge. If you want to go, just say so and go, if anyone gets left behind its their tough luck."

Taking his advice, literally, I announced my intention to leave in five minutes and, when the time was up, I rose and said. "Right, let's go."

There were cries of protest, but I walked out and fired up the engine. St Ledger, Whiteman and McGrogger wandered out and clambered aboard. Slowly I reversed out, but there was still no sign of Mac Wymess. Pulling the steering wheel round I started to edge forwards.

"Come on Mac," came the pleas from the back.

As we slowly moved past the veranda Mac staggered into sight waving a frothing beer mug.

"Hold on, I've just got a fresh pint."

"Too bad," I retorted.

He hesitated for a moment and then thought better of being stranded. Willing hands hauled him aboard and we were away. So far as I was concerned the next stop would be Salisbury. I ignored their pleas to stop in Hartley and, glancing in the mirror I could see that yet another bottle of brandy had miraculously appeared. Passing the village of Norton on the left, the rail crossing red lights were flashing and a diesel locomotive with its crocodile of goods wagons slowly rumbled across the road ahead of us. I slowed, not wanting to stop, when I heard another shout from behind.

"Rod, stop a moment, we want a pee."

"Not a chance," I replied unsympathetically.

By now the crossing was clear so I increased the speed. Lake MacIlwaine lay behind the hills to our right and we joined the weekend traffic of fishermen, sailors and day trippers returning to Salisbury. I glanced in the large door mirror and took a double take. The four boozers were standing in line at attention, relieving themselves over the side of the truck. As they swayed in the breeze, the air stream sprayed a haze of urine over the line of cars behind.

"Bloody hell," I muttered under my breath and prayed that there was no one around who knew me.

At last the Salisbury skyline came into view. My initiation into the transport section, thankfully, was almost over.

CHAPTER 7

Settling In

My next assignment came a few days later when four of us were instructed to go to Kotwa, which was just a dot on the map, and recover the building materials of an abandoned base camp.

Three Nissan trucks and one Isuzu stood waiting. The other drivers quickly appropriated the Nissans and, unsuspectingly, I climbed into the Isuzu. We drove out of Salisbury up the Enterprise Road heading north for Mtoko, 140 kilometres away, and thence to Kotwa, close to the Mozambique border. It was soon evident that, once again, I had unwittingly taken the slowest vehicle. (I had a lot of tricks to learn about this transport unit). The Nissans were quite capable of cruising at 120kph, in their overdrive fifth gear, whereas the Isuzu was barely capable of 100kph. Soon they were out of my sight and the comfort of the lush and verdant farmland soon changed to the more hostile dry bush. The road stretched through the scrubland ahead like a grey ribbon, with the heat causing a watery mirage on the horizon where tree lined, rocky outcrops danced in the reflection.

We had arranged to meet at the small town of Mtoko, where we could stretch our legs and quench our thirst. Unfortunately, I arrived as the others were finishing their drinks and, as they were impatient to leave, my stretching and quenching was very rushed. The others headed off for Kotwa, with my underpowered Isuzu vainly trying to keep them in sight. Inevitably, I was soon alone again, which made me feel uneasy, because, with each kilometre, I was getting closer to the border and I wasn't too sure as to where my exact destination lay.

The surrounding countryside was still and quiet. There was no traffic, no sign of life, with only the occasional remains of deserted kraals to break the desolate landscape. The thatched roofs of the huts were caved in like inverted umbrellas, with the walls choked with weeds and grass. We were well into the operational area now and, as if to confirm my fears, I passed the burnt out shell of a car at the side of the road. My heart skipped a beat as three helicopter gun ships swooped into view, flying low and in formation towards the road like giant wasps, the sun flashing off the domed glass windscreens and glinting off the cannons and shell cases. Smoke ominously drifted up from a thicket of trees ahead.

Apprehensively, I slowed to negotiate a curve and suddenly, appearing on the left, was the remains of the base camp we had been sent to dismantle. The three Nissans were parked in the shade of the trees with the drivers and labourers, unconcernedly, loading wooden beams and corrugated iron sheets, with smoke lazily spiralling into the blue sky from a pile of rubbish burning in a corner.

I parked and, trying not to show my relief, started to load up my truck.

*

I was beginning to get used to my one or two day commitment and the next assignment was to a new base camp being constructed a few miles south of Buhera, a small village situated in a remote area. The closest town was Enkeldoorn of which, it has been said, the biggest attraction was the road leading out of it. Our job was to take in four trucks loaded with building materials.

On reporting for duty I found that one of the drivers was Skalk Van de Merwe, the friend I had bumped into on my first call up and who had sown the seeds in my mind to join transport section in the first place. I was also introduced to Barry Talbot, with whom I was to share many subsequent call ups and who would become a very close friend.

Our instructions were to drive through to Enkeldoorn and await an armoured escort vehicle to lead us in to, what was reported to be, a very dangerous area.

On our arrival at Enkeldoorn we reported to the police station where, it came as no surprise to discover that, nobody knew we were expected. Consequently there was no escort vehicle.

Whilst we sat around awaiting a decision from the mighty military machine, we noticed water dribbling from one of the back wheels of Skalk's truck. As one of the protective measures against land mines the tyres of all military vehicles were three quarters filled with water. The theory being that the water absorbed approximately twenty five per cent of a landmine blast so, although the steering on these vehicles became very heavy, the subsequent protection was invaluable. However, the fact that water was leaking on Skalk's truck meant only one thing. A puncture! We rummaged through all four trucks and eventually managed to come up with one jack and a wheel spanner. The wheel spanner however, had been cunningly designed so that the leverage required to loosen the wheel nuts was considerably longer than the length supplied by the spanner. The obvious solution was to extend the leverage so we searched around for a suitable length of pipe. After a quarter of an hours search, with no success, we congregated around the truck to discuss the problem. It was then that we spotted, half hidden in the grass alongside us, several steel telegraph poles. We hauled one out of the tangle of grass and weeds and surveyed the thirty foot length, which was capable of lifting the whole truck, let alone loosening a few wheel nuts. Nevertheless we had no option and soon it had been slotted on to the end of the wheel spanner, with two of us struggling to lift it through a two metre arc, which had the effect of moving the wheel spanner just a few millimetres. Still, it was enough to crack off the tension on the wheel nut and soon the wheel was changed. We felt quite satisfied with our ingenuity. However, time was passing and we were getting no further on our journey. We wanted to get moving.

At this stage of the war we drivers were totally unarmed, we had a chat and decided that, as obviously, no armed escort was ever going to turn up, we would drive on anyway, without protection, but in close convoy. After many kilometres of twisting, corrugated dirt roads interspersed with occasional muddy quagmires we made it through the inhospitable countryside, unharmed, to the small administration centre of Buhera.

We reported at the police station where, this time, we were expected and an escort vehicle was waiting to lead the way to the construction site. The road now deteriorated to no more than a track, dotted with shallow craters, which was grim evidence of previous landmine explosions.

Eventually we reached our destination, which was a clearing of a few acres, surrounded by low scrub, with a few tents for the labour force and trenches with sandbagged machine gun posts. I didn't envy the troops operating from this camp, but it was pointed out by the escort driver that we had problems of our own. As there was no other road back to Buhera we would have to retrace our steps. For safety reasons we should have tried to return by a different route because, if any terrorists had seen us driving into the area, they would know we had no option but to return by the same route and the chances were high that we could expect an ambush. He cheerfully informed us that, at that very moment, landmines might be being planted, and that by now, it was late afternoon, the perfect time for trouble.

One of our options was to travel at no more than 30 kph, as stipulated in the training manual. If a landmine was detonated at that speed, depending on the weight of the vehicle, hopefully it either got blown over onto its side, with the reasonable chance of the driver sustaining only minor injuries or, if lucky, only a wheel would be blown off. In addition to the water filled wheels, the trucks at that time were protected with heavy steel plating and reinforced rubber matting under the front wheel arches to absorb blast and shrapnel. Later they were totally re-bodied with a heavy steel cab, designed to deflect blast, incorporating thick steel hatchways and a bullet proof windscreen.

During the opening stages of the war, horrific stories were bandied about of drivers who thought that high speeds would get them over and past the landmine before it detonated. Unfortunately that was a fallacy and the subsequent accident, with the vehicle cartwheeling through the air, caused numerous deaths and serious injuries. Conversely, the slower speeds laid the driver wide open to ambush and, in particular, the horror of being on the end of an RPG rocket.

By now the sun was glowing red on the horizon, so we decided to throw caution to the wind and made a collective decision to take the risk of ignoring the 30 kph limit and drive fast to avoid ambush.

With the vehicles unloaded we retraced our steps and lurched, crashed and shuddered those trucks just as fast as they could go for the returning, heart stopping, kilometres. Each darkening bush and rocky outcrop looked more sinister than the last. At one stage Skalk almost lost control as his truck skidded sideways, the wheels scrambling to gain a grip but, with a superhuman effort, he regained control of the lumbering 10 ton beast and carried on.

At Buhera we parked the trucks in different positions within the security fenced compound so that, if there was a raid that night, we would be unlikely to have all the vehicles immobilised. We slept fitfully, but our luck held, the night remained quiet and the run back to Salisbury was uneventful.

*

One thing that always amazed me was that, despite an almost total lack of communication between departments, the military machine did keep, inexorably, moving on.

It was not unusual to be sent somewhere to find someone who nobody had seen, or to collect something that nobody knew about, when you weren't expected in the first place. More by luck than judgement though, the transaction would eventually take place.

To illustrate this point, there was an instance when a Land Rover was handed over to me with orders to take three newly trained recruits to Sinoia, a small town 120 kilometres north west of Salisbury. Three fresh faced youths in shiny new uniforms were waiting and we all climbed aboard. As we drove out of Morris Depot, the youngster sitting next to me turned and asked, "Can we go round to the police hostel on Baines Avenue Sir?"

"Why's that?" I queried.

"There's another recruit to pick up Sir," came the earnest reply.

"Oh, the first irregularity," I thought, but I was rather amused to be addressed as 'Sir', for technically reservists held no rank.

After chasing up the missing recruit our journey recommenced. As we headed out on the Lomagundi Road the lad next to me turned once again and asked. "Do you know where we are going Sir?"

"No, I don't," I replied. "I've been told to take you lot to Sinoia and that's all."

As we drove along, the conversation revealed that the recruits were as ignorant as I was as to their eventual destination. The day before, they had been told to pack their kit and report to the transport section. As we entered Sinoia the most logical course to take was to report to the police station, however, there were blank faces when we enquired at the main desk.

"Try the HQ building round the corner," came the helpful reply.

This we did, but the policeman in reception was none the wiser.

"Wait a while and I will try to find out."

Eventually, after being passed from office to office we struck lucky.

"You shouldn't have come here," the Police Inspector ensconced behind the desk said sharply. "You're supposed to be at the airport."

"Where is that," I enquired, slightly annoyed at his attitude.

"It's just up the road, you can't miss it," he replied abruptly and with that he chivvied us out of his office.

To avoid further complications I stopped at the main police station again and received correct directions to the airport, without which we would have never found it. The airport turned out to be a grass air strip, indistinguishable from the surrounding grassland. One small ramshackle wooden hut stood to one side with a nearby windsock hanging limply in the heat. Not a soul was to be seen and, for the next hour or so, we kicked our heels awaiting further developments to the day's sorry saga. Eventually, a light aircraft landed and taxied to a rest close by. Our problems were not over though, as I discovered that only two of the recruits were expected, their destination being a base camp near Lake Kariba.

"Two down, two to go," I thought, as we retraced our steps back to the HQ building, where the whole process started again.

With a feeling of deja vu we returned to the officer responsible, who sighed with exasperation over these block heads sent from Salisbury.

"A vehicle should be waiting at the main police station entrance, hurry up or you'll miss them!"

I had a feeling that no vehicle would be there, and I was right, the road was deserted. By now I was feeling very exasperated by the situation so decided that, as it was nearing lunch time, we would go down to the troops canteen for a snack and sort things out later. As we approached the canteen, lo and behold, parked in front stood a police vehicle - waiting for our two recruits.

"Where the hell have you been?" asked the driver. "I've been waiting here for ages!"

There was no point in explaining.

Subsequently, I did this run regularly for a number of months, but carefully avoided going anywhere near the HQ building.

Shortly afterwards I discovered that there was a technical term that covered these slight hiccups to the smooth running of the military machine. SNAFU, an Americanism which, when translated reads 'Situation Normal, a Fuck Up'. From then on the phrase 'Situation Normal' was heard many times and clearly understood.

*

On many trips, to brush up my radio procedure, I would cover mile after mile reciting the phonetic alphabet but I still had difficulty in attuning my ear to the crackling, distorted voice emanating from the speaker. For practise, I occasionally re-tuned to the local police wavelength, when entering a town, to try to decipher the conversations.

On one occasion, when approaching Salisbury from Sinoia, I changed to the local frequency to hear if there was anything to listen to. What came through were various references to cars and registration numbers. I realised that I was listening to a conversation between the members of a police speed trap. On rounding a curve I espied a number of vehicles, stopped on the opposite side of the road, with policemen writing out tickets.

With a sense of mischief I leant over and pressed the broadcasting button on my radio microphone. This had the effect of blanking out any conversation in the immediate vicinity. With my finger held firmly I drove the next half a kilometre or so until I had passed the radar equipment, half hidden in the verge, before releasing my hold. The radio crackled back into life.

"................ do you read me? Victor Three, please come in, what the hell's wrong with this radio?"

"This is Victor Three. I'm reading you, loud and clear now, there was interference for a few minutes."

"Roger, Victor three, a bloody army truck just drove through the other way, I bet the bastard blanked us."

Suppressing an inward giggle, I turned off the main road and made my way back to the camp via the back roads.

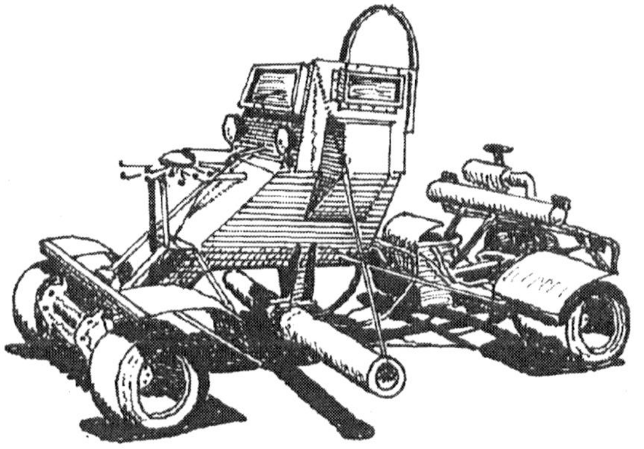

CHAPTER 8

Katiyo

With the collapse of the Caetano Government in Portugal, and the subsequent rapid decolonisation of Mozambique, the border war increased dramatically. Hundreds of miles of hitherto unmarked border were now prone to easy incursion from Mozambique, where the ZANU forces of Robert Mugabe had soon established base camps, under the benign eye of the new government and Frelimo forces of Samora Machel, the President.

During 1976 this Eastern Border saw, not only an increase in terrorist activity but also some cross border clashes between our security forces and Frelimo. This meant that a number of farms, tea and coffee estates, in these regions, required protection out of all proportion to their size.

When the Portuguese had administered Mozambique the control of cross border traffic, by the local population, had been very lax. In many places the tribes were the same on either side of the border so the invisible line laid down by the white settlers, in the nineteenth century, was largely ignored.

With the change of government in Mozambique, however, and the increase in border skirmishes, the Rhodesian government set about constructing a double security fence, laying minefields and, where this was impractical, deploying troops to patrol and protect the area.

Katiyo tea estate was situated in one such area, near the Eastern border, and one Tuesday morning saw me driving to the battle camp, near the citrus estate in the Mazoe valley, some 40 kilometres north of Salisbury. We were collecting thirty field reservists who were keen and eager to get going after their two day refresher course.

We were using two Nissan trucks with trailers and soon we headed back through Salisbury and sped on to Umtali where we arrived in mid afternoon.

As members of transport section we were allowed a certain amount of freedom, compared to the conscripts we chauffeured around. They were confined to the police camp where they dined and slept in large marquees whereas we, on the other hand, could sample the delights of a local hotel. Our only requirement, being to report back for duty the following day at a specified time.

The next morning, refreshed from a good nights sleep, we returned to the police camp to pick up our bleary eyed passengers. Although Katiyo had had a small military guard for some time this was the first time a much larger contingent was to be deployed and, as this was the inaugural run, the Sunray (Officer in charge of operations) for the Umtali area decided to come along to see how things went.

He travelled ahead in a Land Rover and soon we were climbing up towards the Inyanga mountains. The views from the road, as it wound up and around the foothills and valleys, were spectacular and at any other time would have been most enjoyable. As it was, a great deal of concentration was required to negotiate the trucks over this terrain, so consequently there was barely a moment to snatch a brief glance at the impressive vistas.

Whilst passing an area where a great number of African kraals were scattered over the surrounding hillside, I negotiated a series of bends to find the Sunray's vehicle stopped opposite a general store, which was burning fiercely. The local villagers excitedly told us that the store had been ransacked and rocketed only minutes before we arrived, but of the attackers there was no sign. We scoured the nearby terrain through binoculars but the terrorists had vanished amongst the trees and granite outcrops. Sunray reported the devastation over the radio and then, as there were no injuries or fatalities, we left the smouldering ruin and moved off with the reservists, now fully alert and itching for some action.

However, they were to be denied any excitement and, after a few more kilometres, we turned onto the Honde Valley road. As I was still disenchanted by the thought of landmines, I was greatly relieved to find that the road had been recently tarred and we entered the spectacular pass that drops some 500 metres to the valley floor below. The road was so steep in parts that, even after engaging bottom gear, we had to apply the brakes hard to stop the heavy load running away. At the bottom of the pass we stopped to allow engines, clutches and brakes to cool. The smell of burnt asbestos was pungent in the clear air. Unfortunately, the tarmac soon petered out and we were back to a dirt road, Honde Valley had an unenviable reputation for landmines and ambushes which I hoped not to experience at first hand.

Soon we came to the Joint Operations Centre (JOC) which, at first sight, appeared to have been transplanted from the American wild west, with wooden buildings enclosed by a palisade like a US cavalry fort. The effect was further enhanced by a sign bestride the entrance proclaiming 'Welcome to Dodge City'. However, this referred to dodging the numerous bullets and missiles fired at it during a number of attacks in the past.

We seemed to wait an age for Sunray to complete his business and there were impatient mutterings from our passengers, which changed to mutterings of relief as a Pookie mine detecting vehicle appeared from the direction in which we were to travel.

A Pookie was a strange looking vehicle, based on VW mechanical parts, with a narrow, blast protected single seater body, slung between four incredibly wide wheels, incongruously shod with formula one motor racing tyres. Beneath the cab, and stretching the width of the vehicle, was a mine detector. The theory was that, due to the design and the use of such wide wheels, the weight would be distributed more evenly over the surface of the road, thus hopefully not having enough force to activate the detonator on a landmine. All the while the driver would be alert, listening through the headphones for a tell tale sound from the mine detector.

How successful these vehicles were I didn't know, but it was a comfort to have had a vehicle of such wide dimensions check the road ahead.

From where we stood, with the massive granite ramparts of the mountains overlooking the valley with, in the distance, the thin silver thread of Mtarazi Falls glittering in the sunlight, I wondered how long it would be before we could once again wander safely at will around these sights. Many were the times in the past that I had gazed down over the steep drop from where the Mtarazi river plunged out of sight, into the valley below where I now stood.

At last Sunray reappeared and we recommenced our trip deeper into the valley, the vegetation lush and green on either side. With everyone on full alert, we slowly followed the tracks laid by the Pookie, the road hugging the contours of the undulating terrain until, through the trees, we rounded a bend to be confronted by a low level bridge traversing the tumbling waters of the Pungwe river. The bush pressed in menacingly from all sides as we lurched down onto the smooth concrete structure. It was always a heart stopping moment to emerge into the open, to cross a bridge, the vehicles fully exposed, an ideal situation for an ambush, with no escape except the road ahead.

This time we crossed safely, and the road now climbed away from the river towards the beckoning hills wherein were situated a number of tea plantations. We passed the Aberfoyle estate, owned by an Irish company, from which a lovely story – possibly hearsay - had emerged. The head office in Ireland, wanting to improve the social conditions of its overseas employees, decided to construct a golf course for what, on the company records, appeared to be a few hundred employees. What was not realised by Head Office was the fact that there were only about six white employees, the remainder being the local African labourers who had never even heard of the game of golf. Consequently, the six white employees had a full 9 hole golf course at their disposal.

As we climbed higher towards Katiyo, with the land falling steeply away from the roadside, I caught a glimpse of the rusting remains of a wrecked army vehicle lying half hidden below me in the hillside, a previous victim of a landmine explosion.

At last we entered Katiyo tea estate and the road was now tarred and Sunray sped out of sight ahead of us. The thick undergrowth gave way to neat rows of tea bushes. We passed the factory buildings on our right and then the road plunged on down towards another small river. Sunray had vanished and I could see no sign of the manager's house and compound, so I slowed, as the road narrowed down to a sandy track, and I began to feel uneasy as I was sure that somehow we had missed our way. As I stopped close by the river, a Land Rover sped up behind us in a swirl of dust, the driver and passenger gesticulating wildly.

"Turn round and follow us," they shouted. "Hurry up."

I wondered what all the fuss was about but, after turning the truck and trailer with difficulty, complied with their orders and followed them back to an unmarked turning that I had missed, leading to the illusive residence. As we stopped, Sunray came rushing up.

"What the hell did you go down there for?" he queried, pointing towards the river. "Don't you realise that that river is the border with Mozambique?"

Before I could remonstrate with him, pointing out that it was he that had sped away, leaving us no indication of which road to take, he spoke again,

"Can you see that clearing with the tents?" he asked, pointing across the valley where I could just make out some figures moving about. "Well, that is a Frelimo camp and where you drove they quite often come down to the river, and as they are a bit trigger happy, you were bloody lucky."

With that he turned on his heel and stalked off, muttering about the incompetence of police reservists.

I was extremely annoyed by his manner, but was learning fast to keep my mouth shut. This wouldn't be the last time that I came across this arrogant attitude from the regular forces, many of them held reservists in a certain amount of contempt and regarded us as being completely inept at our job. It was pointless to argue the point, because they were the professionals and held rank over us. Consequently, they had the power to make life difficult for us if they wanted to.

After unloading and turning the trucks and trailers around, we were told that we would have to make the return trip on our own. There were no personnel to escort us and we only had two reservists acting as escort protection on each vehicle. Sunray was staying the night there and we were to proceed back to Dodge City where, depending on the time, we might have to stay the night as it would be too dangerous pulling up the pass out of the valley at dusk or later.

Once again, we had the dilemma of either driving slowly, to minimise damage if we hit a landmine, or to drive fast to minimise the risk of ambush. We decided rather foolhardily that we would rather try to avoid ambush and made a dash for it. Fortunately, luck was with us as we bumped and crashed our way along the rough dirt road, retracing our steps across the Pungwe river, until the welcoming sight of the JOC came into sight.

Nobody seemed the slightest bit interested in our query as to whether we had permission to proceed or not so, after weighing up the pros and cons, we decided to make a run for Umtali that evening.

The sun was just disappearing behind the rim of the valley as we set off and, halfway up the pass, I began to have doubts as to our sanity, as dark shadows started to envelope the steep road. At times we were barely moving at a walking pace, the road being at least 1 in 3 in places, but there was no turning back now and, after what seemed an age, we eventually gained the comparative safety of the tar road at the top. It was dark by now but most of the going was down hill and, at times the needle flickered over 120 kph, the diesel governor warning light flashing as we hurtled through the night back to the safety and comfort of our hotel.

I was to complete this trip three more times, each with some incident to recall. Firstly, the route and time changed. Although we always felt that the administrators were faceless and out of touch with those on the ground, our exit from Honde Valley in the half light had been noted, and so the subsequent timetable was altered to alleviate this problem. The first day was unchanged, but on the second day, instead of starting off after breakfast, we would leave Umtali at the crack of dawn, which gave us about three hours start over the previous run. The biggest change however, was that instead of returning to Umtali that night we now, on leaving Honde Valley, carried on deeper into the mountains to Juliasdale where we picked up the Rusape road and thence back to Salisbury, arriving by the late afternoon. The trucks were changed from two Nissans and trailers to three four wheel drive Bedford RM's, two to carry personnel and one for stores.

On one occasion, on arriving at Umtali, we decided to sample a different hotel and drove a few kilometres out of town to Penhalonga and the Aloe Park Motel. The food and accommodation was good and the management even packed some sandwiches for us to take the next day, in lieu of the breakfast that we would miss. Early next morning we stole out of our rooms in the dark and clambered onto the lone RM, that we were using for personal transport. So as not to disturb the other residents at such an early hour we had parked on a slope, the idea being to release the handbrake, enabling the vehicle to roll quietly down the hill and onto the main road. This was not to be, however, as the vehicle wouldn't budge an inch. The Bedford RM has vacuum brakes and, as a safety measure, if the vacuum pressure drops too low the brakes automatically apply. There is a vacuum tank to enable a constant vacuum to be held, even when parked overnight but, unbeknown to us, the tank had a slow leak. The engine had to be started to build up vacuum so there we were, revving the engine at about 4 am, praying that the brakes would soon release to enable us to get back to the police camp. At last the RM started to move, but not before lights had appeared at bedroom windows, with irate faces peering out.

The run to Katiyo went without problems, although my truck, carrying the stores, was once again, far slower than the others. After unloading, I hoped it would be quicker. It was not to be though and, although we stuck together through the mountains, after leaving Rusape on the main road back to Salisbury, the other two trucks soon disappeared into the distance. At one point along the road there was a long slope down to a bridge spanning a river and a similar pull up the other side. As I was getting fed up by now with my gutless wonder, I forced every last ounce of speed out of the truck, as I sped down the slope. 80kph, then 90, the magic 100 and, by a miracle, 120kph. The massive water filled tyres caused the truck to buck wildly but I held on for grim death. A road maintenance gang stared in wonderment as I screamed past when suddenly, there was an almighty bang and a clatter and the truck lost momentum. In the rear view mirror I could see something spinning through the air and so, with resignation, I applied the brakes and stopped at the side of the road. I radioed my plight to the trucks ahead and then clambered down from the cab. Two Africans from the road gang were running down the road with what I recognised as the prop shaft. I peered underneath the truck and, to my horror, saw a gaping hole in the back of the gearbox, aluminium transfer case with black oil dripping out to join the ever increasing pool on the road.

Fortunately, we always carried a tow bar so, for the remaining 150 kilometres, I had the unpleasant and very tiring experience of being towed about 4 metres from the truck in front. We arrived back at the hard square long after dark, the transport section locked up hours before.

On another occasion, I arrived at the hard square to be confronted by my old boozing friends, McGrogger, St. Ledger and Mac Wymess. Like a nightmare you cannot control, we drove to Umtali and discharged our cargo at the police camp. Then we popped round to the Greek Club - just for a quiet drink - drove up towards the Vumba mountains to the Impala Arms Hotel - the manager is a friend of mine - then back to our hotel - for a quick one before turning in – where we ended up with a

small party in the room I was sharing with MacGrogger, whilst I did my best to get some sleep.

The next day, suffering from a combination of hangover and lack of sleep, and with about 12 hours driving ahead of me, I would gladly have been anywhere but there. By a miracle, I managed to get through the day. On the return run St. Ledger, who was driving the stores truck, decided to stop - to wash the dust out - at the Balfour Hotel in Rusape but we plodded on, and periodically he would overtake at speed, for us to see his truck parked outside the next watering hole. The last we saw of him was as he sipped a beer on the veranda of the Marandellas Hotel.

As he was carrying all the men's kit in his truck I made a quick departure when we arrived back at the depot in Salisbury, as the situation started to get a little ugly, with about 40 tired and angry men waiting for their kit to arrive.

CHAPTER 9

Beit Bridge

I was getting used, by now, to the system of volunteering for the various runs at the monthly meetings. I could recognise place names and identify the better routes. Occasionally the name Support Unit came up and I had noticed that it was normally accompanied by groans and a general lack of enthusiasm to volunteer. At that time I had absolutely no idea of what Support Unit was but, taking my cue from the majority, I had carefully avoided volunteering. That was until March when, after the normal lack of response, I found myself volunteered for a run to Chiredzi in the low veldt.

Chiredzi lay in Hippo Valley, where a vast area of virgin bush had been turned into verdant agricultural land, by intensive irrigation, to grow sugar and citrus crops.

Support Unit was located at Tomlinson Depot, which was similar in appearance to an army barracks. The unit consisted of African policemen with white officers and carried out paramilitary duties. As I parked near the obligatory parade ground, I saw a scene of disorganised chaos surrounding a group of vehicles parked nearby. After making a few enquiries, I was directed back to that group where I traced the troop leader in charge who showed me a tatty Bedford RL, lacking doors, as were so many vehicles used in the bush, both for ventilation and for a quick exit.

The loading of the vehicles was a major undertaking, with large gas fired deep freezers, equipment and stores being manhandled into position. For every ten Africans heaving large, heavy supplies on board, there appeared to be ten leaders, each having his own idea of where to push, shove and lift, often in opposing directions, and all the time chatting incessantly while the section officers flitted back and forth with exasperation. After what seemed an eternity we were ready to leave, albeit some hours late and I followed the lead vehicle through the city centre and onto the Beatrice Road, leading towards Fort Victoria.

The group consisted of my Bedford, a Land Rover and a Hyena. The Hyena, used extensively during the war, was a mine protected personnel carrier based on a Ford F250 truck chassis and running gear. Looking rather ungainly, with a V shaped body and bullet proof windows they were, nevertheless, a most versatile machine, being a powerful, four wheel drive, go anywhere vehicle, despite its increased weight due to armour plating.

On arrival at Fort Victoria we lunched at the troops canteen that had moved from its old site, which we had frequented during the Beit Bridge convoy runs, and now occupied part of the hotel in the main street. After refreshment we refuelled the vehicles at the police camp and left the town, passing the afternoon convoy forming up for its run to Beit Bridge.

I recognised familiar landmarks until we turned off at Ngundu Halt to drop into the Hippo Valley, arriving at Chiredzi by late afternoon. The only incident being a mechanical one when my truck decided it could no longer stay in top gear. The last 80 kilometres was completed driving one handed, whilst holding the gear lever back with the other hand.

Our destination was a house on the huge sugar plantation, used as a base camp, where we relieved the troops that had patrolled the area for the last six weeks.

That evening we were entertained by the locals in their sports club and at the crack of dawn I was on my way back to Salisbury with the other troop. It had been an easy run and I wondered what all the fuss was about concerning Support Unit. Lulled into a false sense of security, therefore, the next month I volunteered for another two day run.

Once again I arrived at Tomlinson Depot to the chaos of loading up, but eventually we departed, this time only an hour late, with me driving the now familiar Bedford RL. This time we were heading for Beit Bridge, about 500 kilometres away and, at the meagre speed this old truck could attain, a good eight or nine hour drive. The weather was extremely hot and I was glad of the air swirling around inside the cab.

The base camp was just a few miles before Beit Bridge nestling amongst the dry thorn scrub and baobab trees. We stopped in a swirl of red dust outside the main tents and I climbed down, tired from the heat and the long drive.

"Are you the police reserve driver?" I turned to see a tall, hard looking police inspector striding towards me. From his accent he turned out to be from New Zealand.

"Yes," I replied. "Where do I sleep tonight?"

"You don't," came the curt reply. "We're pulling out now. That's your truck over there!"

"You must be joking," I remonstrated. "I've been driving since early this morning and I'm tired and hungry."

"Too bad," came the unsympathetic reply. "We're moving out now, so you either come back to Salisbury with us or you stay here. I've got enough drivers of my own." With that he turned on his heel and walked off. He knew that I had no option so, feeling very annoyed, I clambered aboard one of the waiting trucks.

"You won't get any change out of Kiwi," laughed the young patrol officer at the wheel. "He can get an extra day on R & R (Rest and Recuperation) if we drive through the night, by the way, my name's Keith."

Calming down slightly, I introduced myself. As we would be confined to the cab for a good few hours it seemed politic to make friends.

The sun was setting as we left the camp to retrace our steps towards Fort Victoria. The African personnel on the back of the truck were in a happy mood, singing tribal songs and, glancing through the rear cab window, I noticed with some concern that large quantities of beer were being distributed. With memories of the 'Booze Cruise' and MacGrogger and friends in mind, I hoped that the drinking wouldn't go too far. Almost as if he had read my mind, Keith said. "Kiwi has treated everyone to beer to celebrate a successful tour. We killed eight ters last week," he boasted.

As the miles passed so the singing got louder. By now it was dark and, by rights, we shouldn't have been on the road as there was a strict curfew imposed in the area.

Approaching Rutenga, which I regarded as being about halfway to Fort Victoria, with our headlights feebly lighting up the ribbon of tarmac ahead, Kiwi in the leading Land Rover suddenly braked violently. At the same time I became aware of something blocking the road. A military vehicle was parked broadside to the road, and as we stopped I observed soldiers ahead, rifles trained on us and, half hidden in the verge, machine gunners taking aim, the ammunition belts glinting in the moonlight.

Kiwi gesticulated angrily, as he argued with the officer in charge, who ordered us to turn into the Rutenga JOC, where a large army camp was situated. Keith looked at me and, shrugging his shoulders, followed the Land Rover up to the Admin. Block. We were herded into the HQ buildings and Kiwi disappeared with a Major.

It turned out that the sound of singing, which from a distance sounded like chanting, had carried through the still night air and the army thought that some drunken terrorists had hijacked a vehicle and were driving along the main road. Instead it turned out to be our trucks full of drunken policemen.

With the curfew enforced, nobody, civilian or military, should have been driving up the road without permission and Kiwi, in his wisdom, hadn't thought to inform anyone of his intentions. With later involvement I was to find out that Support Unit was a law unto itself anyway.

"You're bloody lucky," said a soldier standing nearby. "We were under orders to shoot if there were any doubts as to who it was, you'll have to stay here tonight. There's no way our boss will let you proceed now."

I was relieved that I might get a bed for the night after all, but I hadn't reckoned on the resilience of Kiwi who, on reappearing, shouted, "Back in the trucks, we're carrying on."

I couldn't believe my ears as I dejectedly climbed back up to my seat. Kiwi sped away ahead of us and Keith said, "He's off to see a mate of his and we'll meet up again at Fort Vic."

I decided to get some shut-eye but sleep was to allude me as, not only was a very cool breeze swirling round the cab, but just as my mind drifted away I would jerk awake, as I felt as though I was about to fall through the open doorway.

It was with very tired eyes that I gazed upon the lights of Fort Victoria as we entered the main street. Keith seemed a little bewildered and we stopped. After a conversation with the other drivers it turned out that they had no idea where the police camp was to refuel.

"Well, I can help you there," I said. "Follow me."

Taking over the controls, I drove up to the familiar refuelling post that I had visited every day for two weeks when I was on the convoy.

After filling up we then drove back to the main street to await the arrival of the errant Kiwi. By now the troops, that we were carrying, were becoming slightly the worse for drink. One of our passengers was becoming abusive and soon an argument broke out. Fortunately, a Sergeant Major intervened and quietened things down. It was to be only a temporary lull though, as at that moment two Africans strolled down the street, dressed in civilian clothes, and, after a few enquiries, admitted to being members of the Rhodesian African Rifles, their barracks being only a few miles further along the road.

There was some good-natured banter between the members of the two units until our bolshie friend decided to intervene.

"RAR are a bunch of bloody shits!" he cried.

The two soldiers stopped and turned. "Support Unit are wankers!"

With no other invitation being needed, about twenty African policemen leapt off the trucks and started to chase the soldiers down the street.

Keith and the other officers rushed off to stop what could become a massacre. Fists were already flying. The sergeants also intervened and, before too much damage was done, the fight was stopped. As the rabble climbed back up onto the truck, one of the RAR soldiers insisted on having the last word. As the insult rent the air, so I heard the sound of a rifle being cocked. It was our trouble maker gone berserk. As he aimed it in the vague direction of the soldiers, a Sergeant Major grabbed him from behind. The rifle swung round wildly whilst the drunk shouted almost incoherently in blind rage, "The bloody shit, I'll kill him, the fucking shit!"

As I was sitting in front of him in the cab, which was too close to the firing line to be comfortable, I dived out of the open door and onto the ground. There was a thud beside me and the antagonist lay slumped on the tarmac, knocked out by the fist of another Sergeant who had intervened.

"Let's get the hell out of here," I implored Keith. "Kiwi can travel faster than us so he can catch us up."

Keith reluctantly agreed and moved off, with the passengers now subdued, the only sound was the sobbing of one African policeman nursing an aching jaw and writhing in self pity.

I felt relieved just to be on the move again but after that incident I was wide awake. Sleep was out of the question. We stopped once more at Beatrice with most of our passengers by then lying in an alcoholic stupor. There was still no sign of Kiwi so, after some more persuasion, I managed to get the convoy to move on to the outskirts of Salisbury.

I was glad to be close to home, although it was frustrating to be standing around at the side of the road, in the early hours of the morning, waiting for the missing troop leader. Keith and the officers were reluctant to arrive back at Tomlinson Depot without their troop leader but by now the dawn was breaking and I was cold, tired and hungry. Where was this blasted Kiwi I thought angrily. Suddenly I decided I could stand this disorganisation and indecision no longer.

"Listen," I said angrily to Keith. "I'm waiting five more minutes and if Kiwi isn't here by then I'm taking this truck to Tomlinson depot."

"You can't do that," implored Keith. "Kiwi will do his nut."

"Too bad," I retorted. "I couldn't give a stuff about Kiwi. I've been awake and on the road for nearly 24 hours. This return run has been a complete shambles. I've nearly been shot at twice. I'm tired, cold and fed up. Kiwi is not my boss and he can go to hell."

Keith, silenced by my outburst, seemed to accept the situation.

The minutes ticked by and, as the hand swept round to five minutes, I walked over to the truck then, as I pulled myself up into the drivers seat, by a miracle Kiwi's Land Rover hove into sight.

After taking my leave of the troop at the Depot I decided angrily that I would never drive for Support Unit again.

Vi opened the door, surprised to see me home so early.

"That's the last time I go out with Support Unit," I said wearily and explained what had happened. When I had calmed down she handed me a circular from the Transport Section Leader.

'Dear Rod,

As we are finding it difficult to make up the required days per year, the transport unit are starting two week call-ups with Support Unit, starting next month. Please let me know which dates are clear for you so that I can start working on a rota system.'

CHAPTER 10

One-Five-One-Alpha

With more and more working time being lost, due to both mine and my staff's military commitments, it was becoming quite evident that it would be commercial suicide to continue trading so, after much soul searching, Vi and I took the agonising decision to close down our business.

Due to the lack of confidence in the future, brought about by the gradual escalation of the war, it was impossible to sell the garage as a going concern so the distasteful task began of selling off the equipment. Because of the shortage of new machinery due to trade sanctions, it was easy to sell garage equipment. It was heartrending however to see the workshop, which I had built up over the years, being stripped bare like a skeleton, plucked clean by vultures. Fortunately, I was to miss the final humiliating week of closure because the first of my two week call-up periods started with Support Unit, so the final closure was handled by Vi, who was also a partner in the business. Actually, the closure, although heartbreaking, was not as bad as it could have been, we were not closing because we had gone broke, but because we could see that we would go broke if we carried on, so we didn't have angry creditors knocking on our doors. Every small trader in the country was in the same position as me, so people understood completely. We had both managed to procure good jobs, so at least we had continuity of earnings and consequently no immediate financial problems.

My first two week stint with Support Unit was to be spent at a base camp, known as One-Five-One-Alpha (151A), situated about 20 kilometres north east of Rusape on a farm lying just off the main Inyanga road. The principal areas that the unit patrolled were the Chiduku and Makoni Tribal Trust Lands and the adjacent farmlands.

Support Unit was a front line unit and its job was to track, capture or kill terrorists. It was usually kill as it was a bit difficult to detain somebody wielding an AK47 assault rifle. Patrols would go out for about five days, set up observation posts (OP's) on one of the numerous granite kopjes or gomos, as the larger hills were known, and simply wait and watch for any suspicious movement. Sometimes the OP would be combined with troops sweeping through the bush trying to funnel suspects into view from where a contact could be instigated.

The unit could also be called upon to carry out a follow-up operation after an incident, like a farm attack or murder, to track and hopefully apprehend the culprits.

As a transport driver, my job was to deploy troops into the bush within walking distance of their O.P., to pick up troops after their four or five day tour and to move troops rapidly to a suspect area or even during a contact. One of my more gruesome tasks was to transport victims to the nearest police station or morgue.

On this first call up I was teamed up with Barry Talbot who had already completed one tour of duty at 151A. We had previously met on a Buhera trip and, subsequently, were to do a number of call-ups together, when we forged a friendship of the type that can only be cemented when people are thrown together in times of conflict.

We met up at Tomlinson Depot and Barry introduced me to Inspector Des Mclean, a cheerful extrovert, who was in charge of Support Unit transport. He showed us the Land Rover we were to use and, after collecting the post, equipment and supplies, designated for 151 Alpha, we proceeded to Morris Depot. Here we were issued with our weapons, which were two Uzi sub machine guns, and our two weeks supply of rations from the Quarter Master's Store. Then we were off, heading east on the main Umtali road.

My nerves were tingling with apprehension as this would be my first experience of the real war, working with professionals and possibly coming uncomfortably close to the terrorists themselves. With my minimal training, I hoped that I would cope and not disgrace myself and the Field Reserve.

Mixing Field Reserve drivers with the professionals of Support Unit was an experiment instigated by Des MacLean. It was hoped that the percentage of accidents and damaged vehicles, caused by the enthusiastic young troops, would be reduced by bringing in older and, hopefully, more mature drivers.

In the distance we caught our first glimpse of the rugged Inyanga mountains as we passed Headlands, and on arriving at Rusape we turned left to leave the town on the narrow tarmac road for the last few kilometres of our journey. This road had once been a strip road, so called because of the wheel wide strips of tar laid down like railway lines through the bush by the unemployed during the depression of the 1930's. In later years the gap between the strips had been filled in but, because the road was so narrow, it was still necessary to drop the nearside wheels onto the dirt when passing an oncoming vehicle. Even though we were ostensibly on a tarmac road there was still a danger of a landmine being placed on the verge.

After a few kilometres Barry slowed and pointed to the left, where the khaki canvas tents of a camp could be spotted through the trees. Turning onto a farm track we drove down an avenue of jacaranda trees and past the main farm buildings until we arrived at the camp itself. A white plastered, corrugated iron roofed cottage overlooked a couple of dozen tents arranged in a square formation around the circumference of what, at one time, would have been the lawn of the farm managers dwelling. A volleyball net dominated the centre of the sparse grass and, between the tents and the open bush, lay deep trenches with sandbagged machine gun posts at each corner.

Making our way to a large square tent, within the enclosure, which was to be our home for the next two weeks, we were greeted enthusiastically by the two drivers we were to replace, keen to return to the bright lights of Salisbury. There was a little light banter from them regarding the hardships to be faced and then they left in a flurry of dust.

Without further ado, we entered the cottage and made our way into the ops room to meet the Officer in Charge. Superintendent Fred Mason was a tall, well-built man in his early forties. Handsome and looking slightly younger than his age, with a full head of dark hair, well groomed and greying slightly at the temples. He greeted us and gave a brief outline of the present state of the war in the area.

He was a flamboyant, larger than life character who relished pitting his wits against the insurgents. He had an independent,cavalier attitude that was reflected in the fact that he always used his own radio call sign 'Badger' instead of the more usual 'Sunray' of a commanding officer.

He was so dedicated to his job that occasionally, when things weren't going as well as he thought they should in the field of battle, his frustration would get the better of him and he would shout down the radio mike his favourite phrase. "Get off your butt."

Our tent was sparsely furnished with two camp beds, or stretchers as they were known, a lone wooden table for cooking purposes, a metal folding table and a couple of canvas field chairs.

Being on call 24 hours a day we kept ourselves totally independent from the rest of the camp, and therefore did our own cooking, for which purpose we had two camping gas stoves. Our only luxury was an electric light, which a previous occupant had hung from the centre pole, with the wire precariously looped from the tent top to the cottage roof where it was connected into the main power supply. Because of the amateurishness of the installation we avoided close contact with the metal pole after dark, as it tingled slightly to the touch.

Immediately behind the camp lay the main farmhouse and outbuildings, which still operated as a sheep farm. The house was an attractive, warm, red bricked colonial style house dating from the turn of the 20th century. A wide veranda graced two sides, with the enveloping corrugated iron roof supported by ornate wrought iron pillars.

Behind the house there rose a large granite kopje, the summit upon which was perched a three story, circular,concrete tower. Originally built for telecommunications purposes it now housed the 151Alpha radio base. This kopje was the highest point for miles around and the view from the top was spectacular, having a wide view of tree covered hills and valleys with grey granite outcrops scattered like the ancient ruins of a mythical giant.

It was possible to drive up to the tower and, whenever we had a quiet moment between shifts, we would take a Land Rover up onto the mound and gaze at the view, enjoying the panoramic vision in the pure silence and majesty which only nature can give.

The radio operators lived in the tower, which must have been a wretched existence, shut up in this small building for their entire two week stint. Although they were armed and had a guard, one well placed charge would have brought the whole structure crashing down. It was fortunate that the terrorists didn't seem to realise the damage that could have been inflicted on our radio network and, when it came, the only attack was on the base camp itself, leaving the tower quite safe.

After we had settled in, we took a wander round the camp, and behind a ramshackle garage stood a caravan. As we approached, the door opened and an elderly man in civilian clothes stepped out.

"Hello Van," greeted Barry. "I'd like you to meet Rod."

"Pleased to meet you," he replied in a strong Afrikaans accent.

"Van looks after the vehicles here," explained Barry.

Van, as he was known to everyone, was well into his sixties and should have retired years earlier, but his Afrikaans obstinacy wouldn't allow it. He had spent his life working on the railways as a mechanic, mainly in remote bush areas, and he was determined to do his bit, no matter how small, for the war effort. He was surprisingly fit and agile, and would have loved to have joined the young conscripts on patrol. He was thin but sinewy, his head sparsely covered with grey hair, with keen blue eyes seeming to reflect the vast vista of the African landscape that he had gazed upon all his life time. His skin, tanned dark brown over the years, looked like parchment. Forever dressed in an open necked shirt and shorts he was a familiar figure in the camp. Generous to a fault he would cook us up such Afrikaans delicacies as 'Koeksisters' and present them to us, hot on a plate, as we returned tired and dishevelled after a hard days drive. 151Alpha without Van would have been a bleak place indeed. He had an excellent sense of humour and nothing would get him down. During times of stress it was a great relief to have Van's imperturbability to calm us down.

One day, when still a few kilometres from camp, one of our vehicles broke down. We radioed for assistance and, just by chance, Van was having a cup of tea with the radio operators. Without waiting for an escort, Van shot off in his Land Rover, .22 rifle at his side, and toolboxes bouncing around in the back. Completely ignoring the threat of landmines, within a short space of time he roared into view, enveloping us in a cloud of dust as he screeched to a halt. Pleased to be in the field, he quickly got to work on the ailing machine, his only disappointment being the lack of any action.

His moment of glory did arrive, however, a few months later when in the early hours of the morning, 151Alpha came under attack. As the first explosions from the small arms, mortars and rockets rent the air so Van awoke and leapt to his feet. Groping around in the darkness for his rifle and ammunition, a sudden flash lit up the interior of his caravan. Grabbing the misplaced items he burst out of the caravan and dived into a trench from where he had the satisfaction of expending all his ammunition, although not, unfortunately, as far as he was concerned, causing any fatalities on the other side.

The next morning it was found that although the assailants firing was less than accurate, one of the targets they did hit was Van's caravan. There, just below the roof line, and only a few inches above where Van's head would have been, was a small puncture on opposite walls. The sudden flash of light had been a tracer bullet passing through the caravan.

The only other 'hits' were to the trucks which, parked together in one corner, had come under heavy fire from one of our own enthusiastic machine gunners.

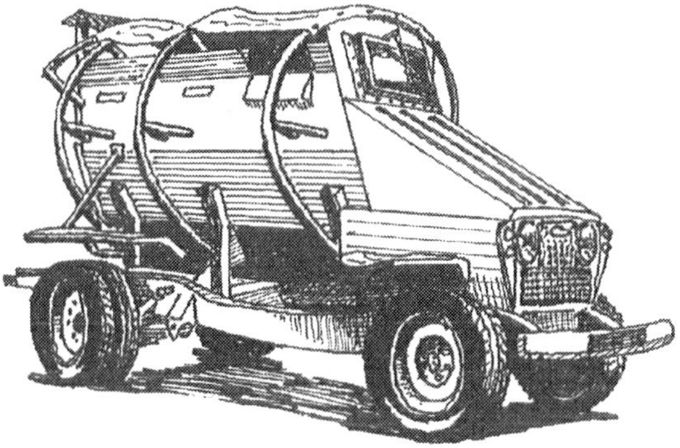

CHAPTER 11

First Deployments

After supper on the first evening we were called into the op's room for a briefing. Crammed into the room were about twenty members of the troop we were to deploy that night. I stood at the back, trembling nervously like a child on the first day at a new school, as the briefing started. There was a description of the whole forthcoming operation, although the only part that was of real interest to us was the area and the map reference point from where we were to deploy the troop. It was a pattern to become familiar in the future. The troop would walk into a designated area from their drop off point and establish an observation post, from which the surrounding terrain could be diligently observed over the ensuing five days.

We retired to the tent to check our maps and, if possible, to get some sleep before setting out at about midnight. Due to my nervous excitement, I could not sleep so I lay there contemplating the job ahead. I would now be driving deep into an area of high terrorist activity where landmines and ambushes possibly lay in store. I remembered the first aid lectures where horrific injuries had been described. Still, Barry was the senior driver on this call up so I would happily allow him to take on the role of 'Mantle Mobile One' the radio call sign of the leading driver.

I must have dozed off eventually, because I awoke with a start as we were roused a few minutes before the departure time. We groped our way blindly through the darkness towards the bulk of the trucks looming ahead. I was strapping myself into the drivers seat of the nearest vehicle when suddenly the passenger door was jerked open and a back pack thrown in. It was closely followed by the troop leader who proceeded to make himself comfortable in the passenger seat. My mind ran over the regulation that forbade passengers from being allowed inside the cab within the operational areas but decided, as a new boy, that it would be prudent to keep quiet on this occasion.

He startled me by saying abruptly. "This is Mobile One."

"No, the other truck is Mobile One," I ventured to correct him.

"Don't be bloody stupid," he retorted with annoyance. "I'm the troop leader, so this is the lead vehicle, now, let's get going."

As we had got off to such a good start, I decided not to argue further and complied with his request, otherwise the situation could have deteriorated into a slanging match.

We drove down to Rusape, turning left in the direction of Umtali until we reached the small settlement of Inyazura where we turned right onto the dirt road leading to Dorowa Mine. There was no moon so the surrounding countryside was totally dark, with just the headlights picking out the scrub and occasional tree next to the unmade road.

After a few kilometres of teeth jarring corrugations, we crossed a narrow low level bridge, spanning an unseen river, and turned left onto a winding track which took us into the surrounding farm land. As it was the beginning of winter my passenger showed no willingness to vacate the warmth of the cab, preferring to take his chance of the risk of landmines.

I kept the speed down to the regulation 30 kph, but this didn't please my companion.

"Christ, can't you speed up a bit? It'll be daylight by the time we get there at this rate."

I ignored him and plodded on until we emerged from the narrow track into an open farmyard surrounded by tobacco barns. Checking his map, while consulting his colleagues in the other truck, he disregarded any advice that I could offer and directed me down another track. After a few more kilometres, we reached some more farm buildings and, after another consultation, the troop decided to debus. The camouflaged figures soon merged with the night and Barry and I were left to work out where we were on the map. Because of the risk of ambush we decided not to retrace our steps, but to follow the track until we came to a recognisable landmark. After following my nose for about 8 kilometres I was amazed when we suddenly emerged at the main tarmac Umtali road. We had evidently driven around in a large loop so, within an hour, we were safely back in the camp.

*

In any war, there is a considerable amount of waiting around between actions and this war was no exception. It was to be two days later, after finishing our breakfast, that we were called into the ops room again. This time a troop, which had been deployed in the field before our arrival, had to be picked up from deep within the Chiduku Tribal Trust Land. Barry led the way in a Hyena, acting as escort, with me lumbering behind in a four wheel drive Bedford RM. We were soon through Rusape and wending our way past Lake Lesapi into the wilderness beyond. The road was in a shocking state of repair, with corrugations like tidal waves, potholes and washaways. We could barely average 10 kph and what, at first glance, appeared to be an easy morning's work, was obviously going to take all day.

The rainy season had been excellent that year, and frequent pools and patches of mud remained which had to be negotiated. After an hour of lurching our way over a myriad of obstacles, testing the rugged four wheel drive chassis to its limit, I suddenly became conscious of lights flashing in the rear view mirror. Unbelievably, in this remote and rugged terrain, a car was trying to overtake. I pulled over and a blue, mud bespattered Datsun bounced past, with an African at the wheel, his wife sitting unconcerned beside him, knitting away, with needles clicking, as if on a Sunday outing. They were totally oblivious to the terrible road conditions that would have tested a professional rally driver to his limits.

I could now appreciate how my African customers could bring their vehicles in for repair with cracked chassis, bent axles and broken springs.

We came across ruts that were so deep, from where the African buses had ploughed through the mud, that when dried out, a car would have straddled the central mound either side, leaving its wheels spinning uselessly in the air, or topple over onto its side.

We had covered, what I considered to be, about three quarters of the way, when we approached the edge of a wide valley where the road wound its way down to a small concrete bridge, straddling a small stream before wending its way up through the trees opposite. Even after the atrocious driving conditions of the previous few kilometres, this was a down hill stretch, the like of which, I had never experienced before.

The road surface of compacted soil had been washed away to expose the unique foundation of the road. The base was constructed like a giant staircase, with a series of stone steps, having a drop of about two feet between each layer. Slowly we proceeded down this stairway with first the front wheels dropping over the edge, closely followed by the crash of the rear axle. Sometimes the edges of the steps would be timed to coincide with both axles dropping at the same time.

In the cab, first there was a shower of dust as the roof lining was head butted, and then a jar to the back as the base of the spine felt the metal frame below the seat spring. Even when we eventually reached the bottom we had to face a similar staircase to get up again. This wasn't quite as bad as, due to the upward incline of the cab, ones body was naturally pushed backwards into the seat, instead of being suspended by the seat belt.

As we crested the rise ahead I breathed a sigh of relief, the road ahead smoothed out with just a few water filled potholes. My relief was short lived, however, as whilst skirting one of these holes the truck suddenly veered to the right and I was thrown violently forward as it lurched to a standstill. What at first sight, had appeared to be firm ground around a muddy pool was, in fact, saturated soil and, even as I unclipped the seat belt, the driver's side front wheel sank with a gurgle up to its axle in soft, sticky mud.

Barry, who was as tired as I was from the sheer physical strain of driving, was not amused.

"Why the hell did you try driving around the puddle?" He enquired angrily.

"I was worried about getting stuck," I replied sheepishly. Words failed him, but the look on his face spoke volumes.

"Before we have any more problems, take a tip from me. Always drive through water on these dirt roads. If the water can't drain away, then the ground must be firm underneath. If you try skirting it, you can see what happens," said Barry, indicating the truck sitting at a crazy angle.

Fortunately, we had shovels with us and for the next hour or so we dug a channel out forward of the wheels, but as fast as we dug the mud out, so the channel refilled with muddy water. Rocks were found to place at the bottom of the trench and we even found some willing helpers, working in a nearby field, to find rocks and bits of wood.Eventually we decided that the big moment had arrived. Barry secured the Hyena to the front of the Bedford with a tow chain that, fortunately, we carried for such emergencies. Taking the strain and with both vehicles in four wheel drive low range, I was pulled clear to the sound of the sucking mud, as it reluctantly relinquished its hold.

By now, we were not just tired, but filthy as well, but we hadn't far to go. The troop that we were to pick up were more than pleased to see us as they had been waiting hours for us to arrive.

Now we turned around and headed back for another dose of physical torture along I road I hoped never to see again. This was the worst stretch of road I was ever to encounter and it was ironic that it should be on my first stint with Support Unit. A month or so later I was to drive through the same stretch again, only to find, to my surprise and delight, that it had been miraculously transformed into a smooth rural road. I believe that pressure had been brought to bear on the local council, by the security force chiefs, to make the area more accessible.

This was fortunate, as the whole area and this road in particular was to become very familiar to me over the next year.

Some years later I was reminded of this jaunt in particular when watching a television documentary about the American 'Truckers', portrayed as muscular heroes skilfully manoeuvring their juggernauts over the highways and byways of the U.S.A. Their air conditioned, power assisted vehicles, driven on smooth metallised roads were in sharp contrast to the four wheel drive trucks with water filled, tractor treaded tyres with no power steering, that we somehow had to force over the rugged African terrain for hours on end in sweltering heat.

*

One day, an emergency call came in from a farm a few kilometres north of the camp. A herd of dairy cattle had disappeared from a pasture and the tracks led off into the adjoining Makoni Tribal Trust Land. We scrambled a tracker and a stick of five troopies and made our way to the scene of the crime. Sure enough, the tracks were quite clear where the cattle had been driven down a dusty road towards the rugged hills and valleys of the Makoni. As the spoor was reasonably fresh, we proceeded with caution, wary of an ambush, but the trail petered out to nothing on a hard granite surface. The tracker and stick debussed to proceed on foot.

Two days later we were called back to pick them up and on our arrival my attention was caught by a pile of charred bones, heads, tails and skins. This was all that was left of the dairy herd. The terrorists had absconded, taking with them as much meat as possible, leaving an aged villager to burn the evidence. Although the villager was questioned, no information could be gleaned as to the whereabouts of the perpetrators of this unhappy saga. Rustling was always an unpleasant affair. The cattle usually died in agony and the rustlers rarely caught. If the troops were known to be closing in, the terrorists would often maim the cattle by hacking off the hooves, leaving the security forces the unpleasant job of putting the cattle out of their bellowing misery as they staggered around on the splintered, bloody remains of their legs. During the latter years of the war cattle rustling reached almost epidemic proportions so a special tracking unit was set up to try to combat the problem.

*

A month later I was back at 151Alpha and on a routine run to Dorowa mine. I was with Barry again, and once more he was driving ahead in the Hyena, whilst I struggled on behind in the Bedford. The road to the mine was fairly wide and, although not tarmac, had a hard shale base which in the normal way would have produced quite a good surface.

Unfortunately, at regular intervals during the day, massive ore carriers pounded the distance between the mine and the railway siding at Inyazura. Consequently the road had become heavily corrugated. Sitting immediately over the front wheels in the Bedford, one felt like a piece of ore in a stamping machine.

Just as my brain felt as if it was becoming detached from my skull the radio crackled into life. I hardly had time to decipher the incoherent jabbering when the roof lining, finally gave up the unequal struggle and, fell on my head, enveloping me in a cloud of dust and fabric. Struggling to control the vehicle and attempting to lift the roof lining off my head, I was about to call up Barry who, I could just see from beneath the obstruction, was still driving sedately in front, when a voice boomed out of the speaker.

"Mantle Mobile One, this is 151 Alpha. Come in please."

"151 Alpha, this is Mobile One, go ahead," replied Barry.

"Barry, what's the situation? Is anyone hurt?" It was Inspector Des Maclean, who was staying at the base camp for a few days.

"Negative," came Barry's surprised reply. "What are you talking about, over."

"Barry, for Christ's sake, don't be a hero, we heard your call for help a moment ago. Give us your LOC (position in latitude and longitude) and we'll get someone to you pronto," by this time Des sounded in a panic. Barry fortunately, coolly intervened.

"Des, nothing has happened to us. I also heard a call a few minutes ago, but it was not us, repeat, it was not us!'

The only drama being enacted, I thought as I fought to keep the enveloping roof lining from obstructing my view, is in controlling ten tons of military truck whilst driving blind.

For the remaining few miles I drove with one hand and, when we eventually pulled up outside the Dorowa police station, I removed the roof lining completely.

There was a hum of excitement around the ops room. It turned out that there had been an ambush on the Wedza to Dorowa mine road, close to where it converged with the Inyazura road. As the crow flies, we had probably been within a couple of miles of the attack.

Within minutes a dusty Land Rover sped into view and an over excited young serviceman leapt out exclaiming wildly about the attack that he had just experienced.

It turned out that he was a member of a Support Unit troop based at 151Charlie, a camp situated in the depths of the Wedza Tribal Trust Land. He had been sent out on a routine run to get stores and had thoughtlessly left without an accompanying escort vehicle.

He had heard the crack of small arms fire, and sped through as fast as possible, but there were no signs of any hits on the Land Rover. On this occasion he had been lucky in only being severely shaken, but he had learnt an important lesson and, when we left, he was waiting for an escort vehicle to accompany him back to camp.

*

One evening we assembled at another briefing. This time we were to take a complete troop into a large ranching area, stay one night and return with the empty trucks the next day.

The ranch was called Romley Estate and, over the years, had gradually been run down to the point where there were large unused areas and it was suspected that there might be a terrorist base or a large arms cache secreted within.

We needed to get into the area as surreptitiously as possible and, whilst scanning the map, we discovered a small track entering the area from a farming community in the south. This was the route we decided to take.

We left the camp with two trucks at about ten o'clock in the evening, with the troop commander leading the way in his Land Rover. Passing the twinkling lights of Inyazura on our right, it was some time before we turned onto the road which meandered its way through rich farmland. Our first problem occurred when we came to turn into the small track which we had so carefully pinpointed on the map. We were confronted by a rusty metal gate, secured by a padlock and chain. After unsuccessfully trying to break the lock, which managed to baffle a full troop of soldiers armed with a variety of weapons, one bright spark realised that the other end of the gate could easily be lifted off its hinges and swung back. We proceeded through the opening, only to find that the track vanished in the long elephant grass that, some years previously, had reclaimed the unused soil.

We pushed on through the grass until the lights of the troop leaders Land Rover illuminated what should have been a low level bridge spanning the rocky banks and sandy bed of a dried up river. The concrete bridge was still intact, but the approach road had previously been washed away leaving a blank end wall about a metre high.

Lights were extinguished and, for the next half an hour or so, we stumbled around in the dark searching for rocks and boulders with which to build an approach ramp. After two attempts the Land Rover pulled itself up onto the bridge, wheels spinning sending stones flying, with the engine straining in low range four wheel drive. The Bedford, having a higher ground clearance with larger wheels had no problems but, no sooner had I pulled onto the bridge, than the engine cut out. No amount of coaxing would start it.

Just then the moon broke out from behind a cloud and there we were, fully exposed, for anyone to see us, with one vehicle broken down and the other, in front, unable to move because, of course, at the other end of the bridge there was a metre drop to the remains of the track below. So much for our clandestine entry to the Romley Estate!

The engine was awkward to work on, being half hidden beneath the cab but, while the rest of the troop grappled with the problem of building another ramp, I traced the fault to the distributor with the aid of a pencil torch and pen knife. It was often handy being a motor mechanic on these trips and I always carried a small emergency tool kit.

As the ramp was finished, so the Bedford sparked into life again and we moved on deeper into the ranch. It soon became evident that, from lack of use, this track had deteriorated badly. There were only a few potholes but what appeared to be a hard compact surface had been sifted by rain, sun and wind so that the top crust was easily broken through for a depth of about 150 millimetres, causing the trucks to strain and push their way through the soft sand. It was fortunate that we were all in four wheel drive as suddenly the Land Rover ahead dropped into a softer patch and, within seconds, it had sunk up to its axles and stopped. With the troops quickly off the back of my truck pushing and straining, it pulled itself clear and I skirted around the sticky patch. However, our problems were still not over, because within a few kilometres my engine cut again. This time from quite high revs, so I knew that the chances of starting it again were remote.

After a short discussion with the troop leader it was decided to leave the truck with a guard around it, whilst the rest of us proceeded to a suitable resting place for the night. The next day we could probably tow it back with the other truck.

Our camp, that night, turned out to be a group of large barns that loomed out of the scrubby bush. They were empty and very dusty so, after placing a guard around the place we bedded down on the concrete load ramp, which was still warm from the daytime sun, that ran along one side of the main building.

Early next morning, after drinking a cup of coffee brewed over one of our small gas stoves, we returned to the crippled Bedford, only to be confounded when it fired up first turn of the starter. Without any more ado we returned to 151 Alpha, leaving the troop to scour this vast area – as it turned out - unsuccessfully for signs of any alien incursion.

The next day was the last of this tour of duty and we were lucky to have no call outs. On quiet days we could get permission to leave the camp environs and spend a few hours in Rusape, shopping or pleasantly relaxing on the veranda of the Balfour Hotel. As this was our last day however, we packed up our personal possessions and sat watching one of the many games of volleyball played between the troops. The night before, there had been a magical moment as we relaxed, knowing that we would shortly be heading home. A group of African troopies had started singing, and their harmonious songs had washed away the tension of war. It was entirely spontaneous and natural, they were not a trained choir, but just had that wonderful ability, so common in Africa,to sing their traditional songs in perfect harmony.

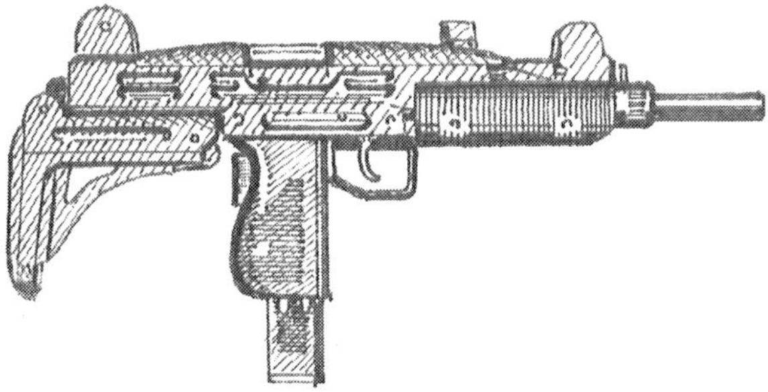

CHAPTER 12

Support Unit Training

During my absence, Vi had finished selling up what remained of our business and finally closed the doors on our old enterprise. Because of the uncertainty of the country's future we were now at the stage of worrying about whether to leave the country or not. We both had good jobs to go to so we decided to hold on for the time being and hope that the government and nationalist leaders would come to an agreement which, up to now, had proved to be elusive.

A letter had been waiting for me on my return, to the effect that I was now permanently seconded to Support Unit and that a training day was arranged for the coming Saturday. I, therefore, joined a small group of drivers congregated in the transport office of Tomlinson Depot. I was pleased to see Barry amongst other familiar faces.

We were shepherded into a lecture room where the Assistant Commissioner introduced himself as the Head of Support Unit and then proceeded to welcome us, as the first reservists permanently attached to the Unit, and gave us a run down of the Unit's history.

Support Unit had originally started in the early part of the century as an African Police Group known as Askaris. Their duties were paramilitary and involved, amongst other duties, the control of riots and paradoxically to guard Government House where the Governor resided. The modern duties were similar except that with the escalation of the war it had become as military as an army unit. After this brief resume the Commissioner retired to let Des Maclean take over. He started by outlining our duties, which were basically to carry out a number of two week tours similar to the one I had just completed. There were six bases to choose from in various parts of the country. Besides 151Alpha near Rusape, there was a small camp to the south in the Wedza T.T.L., one at Mrewa which was a small village to the North of Salisbury, two in Matabeleland in the South of the country with confusingly similar names: Tjolotjo and Tjotjolo and the last near Shabani in the Midlands.

Suddenly there was a shattering explosion and, as we all dived for cover, Des collapsed laughing.

"Just part of your welcome to Support Unit."

Although it transpired to have been a relatively harmless thunderflash, the noise in such a confined space had been deafening and was to be the first of a number of initiation jokes.

"Right, the lecture is over," Des informed us to our relief. "There are two trucks outside so get yourselves up to the shooting range. You don't need any rifles because you are going to have a demonstration of some communist weapons as well as grenades and ant-personnel mines."

With ears still ringing, I clambered up onto the back of the lead truck, thankful to leave the driving to somebody else for a change. As usual a race developed as soon as we hit the open road. Eventually, we were overtaken, accompanied by the jeers from the opposing occupants. Their exuberance was to be short-lived, however, because as we made our way onto the range and turned through a gap in the protective earth bank, two simultaneous explosions hurled dirt and dust over the leading vehicle. With trepidation, we followed through unscathed to laugh as the occupants of the other truck clambered down looking like coal miners, with white eyes and teeth flashing through their grimy faces, as they grinned sheepishly.

The reason for our next lecture was to enable us to recognise the sight and sound of some communist weapons. This was necessary so that in any future contact we would be able to tell who was friend or foe. The weapons demonstrated were the AK47 assault rifle and RPD light machine gun, both ideal terrorist weapons, being light, compact and, in some versions, collapsible to hide away inside a jacket or bag.

As the instructor fired an automatic burst with the AK, so a tingle of memory came back to me. Night time at New Years Gift tea estate and the sound of pebbles on a corrugated iron roof. An altogether lighter sound compared to the heavy thud of our FN's.

Grenades were next and I was relieved to find that we didn't have to throw any ourselves. This being left to the instructor, although even he baulked at throwing the infamous 'stick' grenade that gave as much chance of blowing up the throwers hand, as it did of exploding correctly.

"I've saved the best till last," the instructor excitedly said, seemingly to relish the explosions. "It's one of ours. The Claymore anti-personnel mine. It makes a hell of a bang!"

"Get your heads down for the biggest bang you've ever heard."

We all crouched down behind the protective ring of sandbags in anticipation, as the instructor activated the trip wire. There was a sound like a champagne cork popping and then silence.

"Bugger, it's a blind!" cried the instructor in frustration. "Keep your heads down, that was just the detonator, and the main charge may explode at any moment."

We waited for about five minutes, although the time dragged like an hour. Eventually, after taking a last long pull at a cigarette, the instructor crept out of cover. After a while he gave the all clear and we raised our heads to see a neat barricade of sand bags surrounding the defective item. Hurriedly, we scurried back to our trucks, leaving the instructor to sort out the problem.

Our next training session was covering the Uzi sub machine gun (SMG). This Israeli designed gun was an ideal weapon to carry in a vehicle. Small and light with a folding butt, it could even be fired like a pistol. With 9mm bullets it should have been quite lethal but with an accurate range of less than one hundred metres it was regarded with scorn by the regular forces and dubbed a 'pop gun'. It was probably quite adequate at close quarters, particularly in street fighting but for our kind of terrorist warfare however, something more powerful was preferred. The instructor was a melancholy ex British Army officer who, it was rumoured – although never verified - had never quite got over shooting one of his own men on a training exercise. Despite his aura of sadness he explained the workings of the weapon well and then we retired to a shooting range for practise. We were taught to fire single shots rather than bursts on automatic as this was regarded as wasteful and inaccurate. After we had got used to handling the weapon, our instructor wanted to prove the point.

"Just to show you that firing on automatic is inefficient, I want you to fire off a full magazine from the hip, just like they do in the movies."

We stood no more than ten metres from the targets and let rip with a full magazine of twenty-five rounds. As the pungent smell of carbon and the smoke drifted away we checked our 'kill'. There was no mark on my target and my colleagues hadn't fared any better - so much for the Rambo method!

*

As I became more involved with Support Unit so I learnt more about its makeup and training. Each troop consisted of twenty four men, who carried out a six week tour of duty at any of the main base camps or on its own in more remote areas of the country. The police paramilitary net covered the whole country and their radio call sign 'Mantle' seemed most appropriate, particularly as the insignia of Support Unit was an eagle. One could imagine a giant raptor, with wings spread, like a mantle over the whole country, searching for terrorists.

After completing a six week tour, the troop would then have a weeks rest and recuperation before reporting to the 'battle camp' for a refresher training course, prior to the next six week tour. Listening to the regulars complaining at 151Alpha, we were somewhat in awe of the reputation of 'battle camp' with hard training similar to army commando exercises.

I had already met a young National Serviceman who had allegedly cracked under the strain of the strict discipline. After training with live ammunition he walked out, borrowed a Unit Land Rover and went AWOL to Bulawayo for the remainder of the training period. Misguidedly, he thought he had got away with it when he wasn't arrested on rejoining his troop for the next six week tour. However, at the next battle camp, he was harassed incessantly by the instructors and punished by having to double for the whole week, including carrying his FN rifle with full magazine, weighing almost 7kg, above his head.

There were many times that I saw recruits being punished no longer able to stand, let alone hold a rifle above their heads, tears streaming down their cheeks. To anyone cocooned within a peaceful society, this was abhorrent and I felt very uneasy the first time I witnessed this sort of punishment. Many letters to the press appeared at about this time, complaining of the harsh treatment and other more humiliating punishments, meted out to conscripts.

One famous incident, which raised a howl of protest, was when a squad of reservists in the army was punished for a minor misdemeanour, by having to sit on top of their lockers and sing nursery rhymes until the instructor was satisfied. The only problem was that most of these men were in their late twenties, early thirties and many held high positions in commerce and industry and were not prepared to take this type of infantile punishment without protest. It was counter- productive and caused a lot of ill feeling between the civilians being called up in larger and larger numbers, and the regular forces.

It wasn't long after joining Support Unit that I was summoned to attend a one day training course at the notorious 'battle camp'. On arrival at the Depot a strange sight materialised on the road ahead. Out of the barrack rooms came a large number of troopies making their way to the parade ground. The strange thing was that, to a man, they were all walking with stiff legs on the heels of their boots. Looking like tin soldiers, this weird ensemble gradually made its way to the parade ground to line up in troops and stand motionless. I was scratching my head about this extremely odd behaviour when the truth dawned. Their boots were polished to such a high mirror finish that to walk normally would crack the glaze. To some, as I noticed, it was a wasted exercise when the inspecting officer suddenly shouted at some poor unfortunate individual,

"What's that mark on your boot?"

Instinctively the victim peered down to see the offending mark."Don't look down when I'm talking to you, you miserable excuse for a human being," castigated the officer, "This is the mark I mean," and with that the officer stamped his own boot across the gleaming leather upper.

"Can you feel that mark?"

"Yes Sir," came back the impassive reply, with eyes straight ahead, and no sign of the anguish from throbbing toes and damaged pride.

Further down the line of troops stood one man, in full kit and with gleaming boots, but over the top he was wearing a black plastic bin liner with string around the waist. This caused me a great deal of puzzlement but I later found out that this poor soul had had a black mark against him at a previous parade so, for a set period of time, he had to wear the bin liner dress to show what a 'woman' he was, the ultimate insult to a proud Askari.

Soon our trucks arrived and we had to leave the 'entertainment' to drive to the battle camp, situated in the rolling countryside bordering the Mazoe valley some fifty kilometres north of Salisbury.

We joined 'Whiskey' troop in an old barn converted, with rows of chairs and a blackboard, into a temporary class room. As the lecture got under way, I was taken back to the very first training session I ever attended when we were taught the Counter Vehicle Ambush Procedure. The lecture was spiced up with actual incidents related and then we moved out to a small valley where a practical training ground had been set up.

At first we drivers were separated and given more practise with the Uzi sub machine gun, which had become the standard issue for drivers. We had to fire at moving targets which popped up unexpectantly and then, as our marksmanship improved, we moved on to a mock up ambush situation.

A small charge had been placed to simulate a landmine explosion and each one of us drivers had the task of driving a battered old Bedford RL, with half the troop on the back, down the twisty farm track. As we drew level, there would be a sudden explosion, with a column of dust engulfing the cab. Stopping immediately, as if the vehicle had been disabled, we all had to debus while the other half of the troop, acting as terrorists, would open fire with blanks, simulating an ambush. We each had our own particular position to go to and this was practised time and time again.

On one run, Patrol Officer Smith, who I had met in a previous call up, and who was well known for bucking the system, accidentally tripped over a root whilst in full flight on a charge against the 'terrorist' position and disappeared from view in the undergrowth.

"Get up Smith, and stop buggering about," cried the instructor.

"But Sir, I fell………"

"Don't give me any lip. I know you from old," retaliated the instructor, who immediately put a rather bemused and aching Smith on a charge.

In the afternoon, the training became a bit more serious when a member of the Unit, who was an ex-Vietnam veteran, acted as a terrorist. Dispensing with the landmine explosion and, armed with an Armalite rifle, he commenced firing over our heads from a nearby hill with live ammunition to simulate a straightforward ambush.

At the end of the day, a full-scale vehicle ambush with a counter ambush skirmish was set up, only this time everyone used live ammunition. It was carefully orchestrated by the instructors who knew the angles of fire but, all the same I kept my head as low as possible, sweating profusely.

At the end of the action the troop was lined up, magazines removed and rifles cleaned. After clearing an FN, the trigger is squeezed to relieve the pressure on the firing pin and, as each rifle was cleared, so a metallic click could be heard. That was, until an FN barked a round harmlessly into the sky.

The instructor in charge reacted instantly and harshly. Knocking the African troopie to the ground, he held him face down with a foot on his back.

"Where's a gunner?" he shouted in anger, at which point a machine gunner stepped forward. His weapon was handed over and, with grim determination, the instructor pressed the barrel onto the back of the offender's neck.

"Accidental discharge can kill. You will not A.D. again."

The poor wretch screamed, as the red hot barrel which, until a few moments before, had been pumping out fire at the rate of 2000 rounds a minute, burned into his flesh. Roughly he was pulled to his feet sobbing, rifle removed, and placed under arrest.

I could understand why battle camp had such an awesome reputation because, if you stepped out of line, the punishment was immediate and harsh. The severity of the castigation by the instructor over the AD incident was strictly against the rule book, and we couldn't help feeling a great deal of sympathy for the youngster, but on a later call-up the reasons for the instructor's wrath were to be made horrendously clear.

CHAPTER 13

Fire Force

Back at home, life carried on as usual. It seemed strange that, with the escalation of the war in the open countryside, life in the towns and cities appeared, on the surface, to be almost unaffected. The commercial and industrial pulse of the country had to carry on, with the rush hour traffic still choking the arteries of the cities each morning and evening. Under the surface of the seeming normality however, was the fact that every business had members of staff called up for varying periods of time. To keep businesses running, more employees were taken on so that enough people were working, at any one time, to keep the operation going.

During the early years of the war the companies themselves were responsible for making up the difference between the army pay and civilian salaries but, as the war escalated and the burden on industry increased, the government took over this responsibility. By 1977 my part time commitment had increased to the point where I should have worked half the year for commerce and half for the security forces. As this was broken down into two week call ups, in theory this meant two weeks on and two weeks off ad infinitum. In practise I ended up the year with about seventeen weeks of call ups; approximately one third of the year. Even so there was a total lack of continuity on commerce and industry and it was amazing that life still seemed to carry on, with relatively few companies closing down.

With the terrorist activity getting closer to Salisbury it meant that most people stayed within the city boundaries, rarely venturing beyond unless well armed. The social life boomed as we all drew together under the 'laager' mentality. Between call ups there seemed to be a never ending round of parties, braaivleis, swimming parties, dinners and dances. It was an unhealthy environment for families and the divorce rates soared under this unnatural tension.

I was finding it particularly difficult to bid my family farewell before each two week stint. My two year old son Michael biting back tears and my daughter Susan, although outwardly calm, suffering from nervous alopetia, causing patches of her hair to thin out alarmingly. With the dead and injured being reported on daily in the news it was difficult to ignore the dangers that existed on the regular forays into the bush.

During my next call up I witnessed my first terrorist contact since joining Support Unit. Although not directly involved in the fighting as such, it was still an exciting and very moving experience. Once again, Barry and I were together, but this time we were joined by a third driver, Bill.

Before dawn and under cover of darkness, we took three trucks loaded with troops and penetrated deep into the Makoni TTL, where terrorist activity had been reported, until we arrived at an INTAF fort. Here we met up with the local Special Branch Officers and other local security chiefs eager to get in on the act. As the first signs of light penetrated the eastern horizon we moved off until we came to the edge of a low plateau overlooking a wide plain, guarded by a range of distant mountains. In the valley below was the target village where terrorists had been positively identified.

We parked on the playing field of a church mission school and, as the daylight strengthened, the first helicopters flew into the attack. Through binoculars we could clearly see the first helicopter gun ship open fire. The reaction was like an ant's nest being disturbed. Dark figures could be seen tumbling out of their huts and running wildly away. A helicopter landed and disgorged units of the Rhodesian Light Infantry who were soon in hot pursuit of the enemy.

A lone Dakota aeroplane circled overhead from where the battle below was being directed. We could hear the interchange between the plane and the ground forces over our radio.

"Green Leader, this is Green Three, have ters visual near banana trees."

"Roger Green Three, continue ...." The crackling voice was suddenly lost in a blur of cannon fire.

"............ hut with ters in it, copy?"

"Copied, confirm that they are ters, over."

"Affirmative."

A short burst of gunfire and the tracer bullets set fire to the tinder dry thatched roof of the hut. As figures could be seen running from the conflagration so they were cut down by the troops on the ground.

Whilst the contact was continuing in the distance, the village we were in had started to come to life. The locals wandered about their business appearing to be totally unaware of the drama unfolding in the valley below. A young African woman wandered over to talk to our troops, she was quite relaxed and was laughing and joking with them when the first helicopter with casualties, unexpectedly landed nearby on the playing field.

A wounded villager, with blood streaming from a leg wound was lifted on a stretcher and rushed to one of the Land Rovers. The girl stared with dismay, and beneath her thin dirty cotton dress her nipples hardened from the shock as she stumbled away in tears.

A second Allouette landed and another villager was stretchered out. This time it was an old man, his crinkled hair turned white with the years. A picannin, possibly a grandchild, comforted him, another unfortunate caught between the opposing forces. The man was severely wounded and the medics set up a saline drip but to my untrained eye appeared to be dying. His skin was grey and dull, his eyes unseeing.

I felt what was probably a shock reaction to my first direct experience of the violence of war. I felt deep sorrow for this poor old man, who had to end his days in such a violent way, but I also felt intense anger against the terrorists who had forced this confrontation.

The Alouettes took off with reinforcements of Support Unit troops and when a third landed, instead of wounded, the first captured terrorist was roughly pushed towards us. In that split second, with the severely wounded villager still lying nearby, my anger was such that I had an overwhelming urge to strike this man. Fortunately, I kept control of myself and sat down in my truck trembling uncontrollably.

I realised that I was suffering from shock and sat quietly, breathing deeply. I heard a call for a driver and volunteered, not knowing what I had to do, but just glad to be away from this upsetting scene.

A Land Rover led the way and I followed in its dusty trail until we eventually came to the main Umtali road near Odzi. We sped down the tarmac road for a number of kilometres and then turned up the Inyanga road until we were behind the range of mountains that we had seen from the plateau. Soon we turned into the range on a rough dirt track. We passed the twisted wreckage of a jeep that had been blown up sometime previously by a landmine, then a convoy of army trucks appeared coming towards us. As they passed I caught a glimpse of the sunburnt, unsmiling faces of the regular infantry troops returning to their base. As the road twisted through the range we came upon a clearing in which stood the Support Unit troops. Beside them was a pile of arms and ammunition, bundles of clothes and, to one side, the partially clad bodies of three terrorists. They lay dust covered, blood congealed on wounds, eyes glazed.

They were put into black plastic body bags, similar to bin bags and were, like rubbish, unceremoniously thrown onto the floor of the open Land Rover. This was done by two distressed youths captured as suspected terrorists or collaborators.

The pile of weapons included AK47 assault rifles, an RPD machine gun, hand grenades, land mines and hundreds of rounds of tarnished copper- coated ammunition.

As the arms cache was loaded onto my truck and the troops clambered aboard, the two miserable looking youths looked up enquiringly and asked where they were to sit.

"Sit with your mates," retorted the troop commander unfeelingly and made them clamber into the back of the Land Rover to sit on top of their recently departed comrades.

It had been a long, exciting but, at the same time, upsetting day.

My initiation into the real war of death and distress had shocked and unsettled me. Although war can never be condoned, particularly when civilians are involved I was to learn to live with the reality of what was going on.

As I followed the Land Rover back to Rusape my mind had a lot to dwell upon, whilst the pungent smell of death wafted back in the air stream.

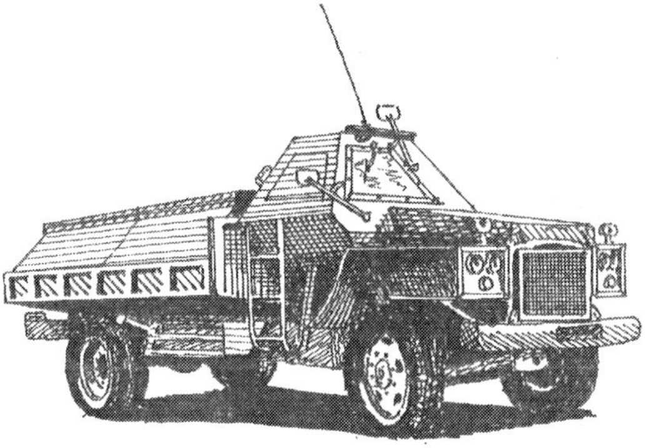

CHAPTER 14

Stand-To

Every morning, before the break of dawn and every evening, after sunset as the dusk enveloped us, the camp practised 'stand-to'. This entailed everyone, at the sound of a whistle, rushing to the trenches and standing alert with rifles cocked, peering over the sandbagged emplacements around the perimeter. There would be absolute silence until a second whistle blast, when we would all carry on normal camp duties.

On my second tour at 151Alpha there were three drivers and, at the appointed whistle we would rush to the nearest sandbagged trench, which happened to be immediately behind our tent, to stand with rifles at the ready in the dawn light, reminiscent of soldiers in the Somme.

On the first morning we were peering through the half-light in the silent cold, that pre-empts the dawn when Bill, the third driver, broke wind. Like a group of schoolboys we collapsed into giggles as the muffled explosions continued, sounding all the louder in the tense silence.

"Quiet," hissed an officer in the next trench. "What the hell's going on?"

To which Bill replied with another volley.

*

It didn't matter in what part of the country I did my call ups, the early morning stand-to was always the most pleasant time of day, and has left me with an indelible memory of the awakening of the African bush. As the daylight seeped through the darkness and familiar trees and bushes appeared through the thin ground mist, so the dawn chorus would start. From the birds in the trees to the lowliest ant on the ground, the air came alive with the resonance of Africa, even the plants seemed to creak a welcome to the day and add to the cacophony of sound.

As reservists seconded to a regular unit, we often felt a gap between ourselves and the professionals. At the worst, we were the butt of derisory comments and at the best, we were tolerated because we were necessary for the troop movements. As time went on we proved that we could do our job as well as the next man, so the prejudices started to decline. On a later call up I was met by Superintendent Fred Mason as I arrived and, much to my puzzlement, he led me over to the trench, behind our tent, where we normally stood for stand-to. At one end, the trench had been dug down about another foot to accommodate my 6' 6" frame. He passed it off as a bit of a joke but, as he had organised it in my absence, I felt that at that moment I had been fully accepted as part of the team.

*

During my first call up with Support Unit we had been driving Bedford RLs and RMs with only limited land mine protection, consisting of water filled tyres and steel plating under the front wheel arches, with heavy rubber matting to catch shrapnel. The only mine protected vehicle we had was the Hyena escort vehicle mentioned in a previous chapter but it was limited to carrying only one stick of four men plus a driver.

On my second tour to 151Alpha we were introduced to the 'Puma'. This was an armoured troop carrier, based on a Nissan 10 ton truck chassis. The cab was reminiscent of a First World War armoured car and the heavily armoured rear could carry a full troop of twenty four men.

The driver sat further back from the front wheels so consequently it was more comfortable to drive and the massive diesel engine was capable of propelling this ungainly mass of steel at a steady 120 kph on a good tar road. Generally we preferred the Puma for the extra comfort and speed but the vehicle did have a number of drawbacks. The brakes were totally inadequate to cope with the extra weight, although an exhaust brake was fitted which was activated by a switch on the dashboard.

Prior to the Pumas, all army and police vehicles had been petrol powered. With the coming of diesel came refuelling problems when at any distance from home base.

The other major problem was that because the Puma was based on an ordinary truck chassis, only with substantially more weight, the risk of getting stuck in muddy or sandy terrain was so much higher without the benefit of four-wheel drive. Sometimes a choice had to be made to switch back to the more lightly protected but four wheel drive Bedford.

The last few days of a call-up couldn't go quickly enough once the bright lights of Salisbury started to beckon. There was a great feeling of relief when the last deployment had taken place and we always hoped to have a quiet last night, pack up early in the morning and await the arrival of the relief drivers.

On my second call-up, the last morning dawned quietly and whilst at stand-to we were talking about the imminent journey home when an urgent call came through for a driver. Unfortunately, being the nearest, I was volunteered to take a troop down to a farm near Inyazura where spoor of a large force of terrorists had been picked up at first light. Having no time for a wash or shave and having had no breakfast, I grabbed my rifle and ammunition and within minutes I was taking our only Bedford RM down the main Umtali road as fast as the poor old thing would go. It had been decided that the Puma might get into problems over the terrain I was likely to encounter.

We duly arrived at the farm to find the local police in a Land Rover and the farmer astride a horse waiting impatiently. With no word of explanation the farmer moved off and we followed at a respectable distance along narrow dirt tracks, across fields and through virgin bush, stopping periodically for the trackers to check the spoor. The tracks were just foot marks in the dust but, what made it unusual, was the great number, probably twenty or thirty pairs, which made an obvious and easy trail to follow in the dirt. The trackers seemed to think that the evidence was only a few hours old and the further we drove into the undulating bush the more wary I became of every blind turn. We had never tracked such a large number before because they were usually in threes or fours.

We were getting into hilly terrain when our path was blocked by an enormous bank about 3 metres high and with no way round it. With a few snorts, the horse dug its hooves in and pulled itself to the top. I eyed the bank with some misgivings. Although I had driven over a great variety of ground in my time, I was dubious as to whether the RM had the power to pull itself up this steep slope.

"Come on," shouted the farmer impatiently.

"I don't think the truck can get up there," I replied.

"Rubbish, just put your foot down," and, dismissing us with that curt statement, he started trotting off.

Engaging four wheel drive and low range I headed towards the bank. As the front wheels bit into the soft earth the cab bucked and I was thrown back into the seat. The windscreen had replaced the roof and, gazing at the blue sky above I kept my foot hard on the accelerator. Bucking like a wild bronco, we slowly but surely climbed upwards until, just as I thought we might topple over backwards, the front wheels crashed down, bringing the landscape back into view.

As I stopped to re-engage normal drive I became aware of the shambles behind me. The troops were sprawled out at the rear of the truck and were struggling to their feet, recovering their equipment. Some had fallen or leapt out of the back and a few packs lay at the bottom of the incline. Fortunately nobody was hurt and, with typical African sense of humour, there were hoots of laughter as they sorted themselves out. The dour farmer was by now far ahead, oblivious of the hilarity behind.

It was a sobering thought that we had forgotten all our training and disregarded all precautions against an ambush. We would have been sitting ducks and it was a lesson I never forgot from then on.

We soon came out into open country and on crossing a vlei, which at that time of year was baked hard by the sun, we lost the tracks of the terrorists. We retraced our steps and checked in an every increasing circle but the spoor had disappeared. Somehow a large number of insurgents had simply vanished.

We called up 151Alpha for instructions and, as usual, there was a lot of humming and haaring over the airwaves. As time was by now marching on, I was getting slightly worried about missing my transport home but, after much procrastination we received the order to return back to base.

*

One night, after a successful deployment, Bill and I were speeding in typical flat out fashion along the last few miles of narrow tarmac road towards our snug beds when, within the poor illumination from our mud splattered head lamps, I realised a number of cows had strayed across the road. Their blotchy black, brown and white markings were a perfect camouflage and, with no time to stop, I swerved and somehow avoided hitting them. My relief was short lived though as over the radio came Bill's frantic call.

"Mobile One, I've hit a bloody cow!"

I swore under my breath, stopped, turned the Puma round and drove slowly back down the road, dreading the gory scene that I felt must meet my eyes.

Bill's Puma stood in the middle of the road, the bumper crumpled against the nearside wheel. The herd had scattered and the dark mound of the injured cow lay on the verge a few metres behind.

I flicked on my pencil torch, dreading the sight that I might see. The cow looked up with a baleful expression, but made no sound. We checked for injuries but, surprisingly, there appeared to be none.

"Let's get it on its feet," I suggested. "If it can walk it's probably OK."

By this time our escort had joined us and between the six of us we pushed and heaved but could not budge the beast, which still made no sound and just sat looking quizzically at us. In exasperation I aimed a kick at her rump.

"Get up you silly cow."

Obediently she clambered to her feet and staggered a few steps before collapsing onto the grass verge again,

"I'll tell you what we'll do," I said, seeing Bill's look of concern."We'll leave her where she is and come back and see if she is still here tomorrow. Then we'll decide what to do."

The next day we had to make a trip to Rusape to collect supplies and as we approached the spot where we had left the cow we could see the inert form still laying there. When we stopped, she raised an enquiring head as we walked towards her. In the daylight there was still no sign of any injury so we decided to leave her for another day.

For the next three or four days an inquisitive face would stare at us each time we slowed to check on her condition.

"It's no good," I said with resignation on our last day. "We can't just leave her there, we'd better try to find the farm it came from on our way home."

There wasn't much enthusiasm from the other drivers as this detour would probably add hours to our homeward trip. We loaded the Land Rover and set off towards Rusape, rounded the curve towards what was now a very familiar stretch of road but the grass verge was empty. We stopped and search but there was no sign of the invalid. With lighter hearts we continued on our way with Bill noticeably more cheerful.

CHAPTER 15

Anecdotes from the Bush

One afternoon, Barry and I, with a new driver Ben, were sitting lazily in our quarters reading, talking and generally whiling the time away. The camp was quiet. All the troops had been deployed. Fred Mason and the Troop Commanders were at a meeting in Rusape, consequently there was a lull in our war. Van had gone off fishing. We were at peace with the world.

Strolling outside I heard something flop from the overhanging tree onto the canvas roof. On turning, I was startled to see a long green snake curl over the edge and slither down onto the grass.

"Snake!" I yelled, and Ben and Barry leapt out of the tent as one. With trepidation we watched it slide past the corrugated iron ablution block and finally disappear into a sand bagged pit which housed our spare gas bottles.

Cautiously we peered into the shady depths of the trench. As our eyes accustomed to the gloom we glimpsed a scaly tail slide out of sight beneath the silver canisters. We called the Sergeant Major over but, at the mention of a snake, he rapidly made himself scarce.

We had decided that the snake was a Boomslang, which is one of the most deadly snakes in Africa. Come what may, that snake had to be disposed of, otherwise life would become very difficult. One could hardly snuggle nonchalantly into ones sleeping bag knowing that you may have an unwanted bedfellow.

A constable was dispatched to call Van back urgently and we set about making up a plan of action. By the time Van appeared we had cut some long poles from some nearby saplings.

"What are you doing?" he enquired.

"There's a snake down there," we replied, pointing into the pit.

"Bloody hell, I'll get my rifle."

We looked at each other aghast.

"Hang on a minute, there are gas bottles down there."

"Don't panic, I have a plan."

He returned within seconds with a small .22 rifle with telescopic sights and laughed.

"This small bore will be safe enough."

Using the poles that we had made, we rolled the gas canisters over until we had a clear view of the snake which was deftly pinned down with one pole.

Van lifted the rifle to his shoulder, squinted down the sight and fired. There was a small crack, the snake jerked and was dead.

Thankfully we dragged the corpse out and hung it over a pole. The African custom was to leave it for a day before coming near and it was still there when Fred Mason and the Troop Commanders returned from their meeting. They came to look at our trophy and, as Fred turned away he nonchalantly said, "You know they always have a mate!"

Startled we scanned the branches of the tree from whence the snake had first appeared.

"Do you think he was joking?" asked Ben. Whether he was or not, needless to say, we slept fitfully that night.

*

One part of the Makoni TTL, to which we occasionally had to gain access, was particularly inaccessible. The road was no more than a rutted track that had been washed away a number of times. It meandered around a range of wooded hills and between large granite boulders which were ideal ambush sites. At one stage we were compelled to drive across open grass to skirt marshland before lurching and bouncing over what was no more than a dried out water course, until what was left of the track petered out at a dilapidated general store.

On one occasion we had arrived to pick up Echo Troop, who had been operating observation posts in the area for the previous week, when we received a radio call from them to the effect that at that very moment they had a group of suspected terrorists under observation in the vicinity.

The only sign of life at the store was a wizened old woman serving behind the counter and a piccanin playing on the dusty veranda.

We spread our maps out to try to locate the spot where the suspects were gathered. Meanwhile the radio crackled through confirmation that the troop were observing four males each armed with AK assault rifles.

For the next half an hour we traced their movements on the map, when eventually an observer, in the hills above, pin pointed a small banana plantation that the terrorists were making for. Checking the map, we suddenly realised that the swaying green fronds some 100 metres behind the general store were the very foliage referred to.

We dropped behind whatever cover was available and soon had our rifle sights trained on the only gap through which they could come.

The wait seemed an age, my hands were clammy and sweat dribbled down my face.

The radio suddenly blared into life.

"'They're running away."

We leapt to our feet and ran for the grove. There was no sight or sound of them. The observation post had lost sight of them and we disconsolately trudged back to the store.

The radio operator was sure that the terrorists had been warned. "They suddenly stopped, turned and scattered."

The veranda was still. The piccanin had disappeared. The old woman was questioned, but she remained tight lipped.

*

A couple of nights before arriving at 151Alpha for one of the many call-ups that I passed there, the camp had come under attack. There were no fatalities, injuries or even damage, but the camp officer decided to tighten our defences. One afternoon our boredom was interrupted by a call to attend a demonstration of the use of a mortar.

A sandbagged enclosure had been built and Mac, an ex-army instructor, stood proudly next to a mortar tube.

First the principles of a mortar were explained and a variety of communist and British bombs displayed. He was evidently in love with his subject and wasn't shy in mentioning his prowess at hitting the target.

"See that down there?" a small patch of water twinkled at the neck of a shallow valley about 500 metres away. With a gleam in his eye Mac dropped the first bomb down the tube. With a hollow explosion the projectile soared through the air to drop slightly short of the target.

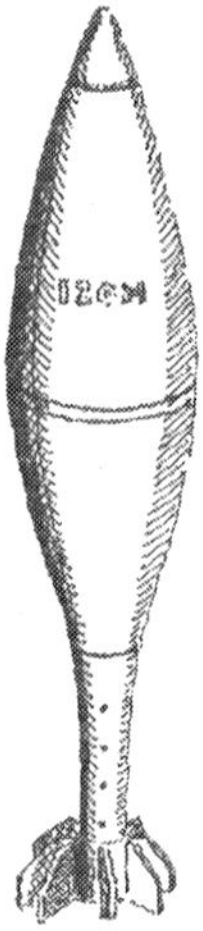

With a slightly more powerful charge he deftly let fly again and we were impressed when a distinct splash confirmed his accuracy. By now Mac had really got the bit between his teeth. His attention switched to a lone pine tree standing approximately 100 metres outside the camp boundary.

Once again, the first shot landed wide of the target but Mac was now in full swing and with a few deft adjustments another bomb sped on its way. Unfortunately though, instead of piercing the air like a rocket, this one tumbled end over end until it landed at the base of the tree in ominous silence.

"Sod it," cursed Mac. "It's a blind. Nobody go near it."

The area was cordoned off and the next morning an army Land Rover arrived, containing a bomb disposal officer.

By laying a separate charge the mortar was successfully detonated, but the drama wasn't over yet. Suspended above the tree were some power lines. The explosion cut the wires which started a small bush fire, quickly disrupting the electricity supply to the surrounding area. The camp was alerted and we spent the next hour beating out the crackling grass and undergrowth.

That night gas lamps and candles flickered their ghostly light throughout the camp and it wasn't until the following day that the engineers arrived to repair the damage.

The C.O. wasn't too impressed by this disruption to his base camp so from then on there were no more practical demonstrations although 'Bomber Mac', as he had now become known, occasionally could be found gazing longingly at the mortar tube now relegated to the storeroom.

CHAPTER 16

Hallucinations

One tour at 151Alpha was particularly busy, with more of our deployments being at about midnight. Consequently, by the time we had returned to camp and collapsed into bed, we were lucky if we managed to snatch 3 or 4 hours sleep.

Tired though I was, I found it impossible to catch up with sleep during the day. One night, when we deployed into the Chiduku area, I was so tired and my nerves were so much on edge that I started to hallucinate. As I peered through the thick, bulletproof windscreen at the landscape ahead, swathed in bright moonlight, a terrorist appeared, assault rifle waving in the air. My heart leapt, my brain lurched within my skull and a split second later my headlights picked out, not a terrorist, but the skeletal remains of a dead tree, leafless branches waving mockingly in the slight breeze.

About an hour later, with my nerves shattered, I thankfully sank into my sleeping bag, but my head barely seemed to touch the pillow when I became aware of a commotion outside.

There was the sound of running feet, the clank of equipment, when suddenly our tent flap was thrust aside.

"Wake up, we need two drivers now!" came the command.

Groaning, I struggled out of my bed. We were all as tired as each other so it was no good hoping that someone else would go.

Ben and I got our kit together and within a few minutes were climbing into our respective armoured trucks.

The troop commander arrived and told Ben that only one driver was needed after all, and ordered his troop into my truck. I couldn't believe my bad luck as Ben made his way back to bed.

Fortunately we had already refuelled when we had returned earlier to camp so there was no delay in setting off. Our orders were to reinforce the 151Charlie troop commander who had been ambushed near Wedza, some 130kilometres away.

Apparently the troop leader had been returning to 151Charlie base camp, ahead of his Bedford RM, after deploying troops into the field that night, when his Land Rover had detonated a landmine. The Bedford, with the road ahead partially blocked with wreckage, had come under small arms fire and in the confusion the driver had unavoidably crashed into a ditch. Miraculously there were no injuries and fire had been returned. All was now quiet but they needed to be relieved from a very delicate situation. With no more transport available at their own camp, where only a skeleton staff remained, we were their nearest base camp to be able to offer assistance. Even so, it took a good two hours to reach the ambush site where we were greeted with relief by the troop commander.

All was quiet, and it was decided to wait until dawn before starting a follow up. We bedded down on the rough stony ground but it wasn't until I found a patch of soft ground that I managed to sleep fitfully until first light, only to discover that I was lying on an ant's nest.

As the daylight filtered through the trees a sorry sight greeted us. The Land Rover, which had been brand new and on its first tour of duty, was stranded forlornly half off the road, with the off side front wheel, suspension and bodywork blown away. The bonnet, still with the spare wheel attached, was found about a hundred metres away in the bush. It was amazing that the driver and occupants had got out without a scratch. The Bedford, peppered with bullet holes, stood nose down in the ditch alongside.

As soon as the light was clear enough, the trackers moved out while the remainder of us brewed up some coffee and then set about the task of pulling the Bedford out of the ditch. We had hardly started when, close at hand, shots were fired. The bush was too dense to see anything and, in the silence that followed we crouched uneasily, weapons at the ready. The radio crackled into life and we learnt that the trackers had almost immediately stumbled upon the terrorist gang who, unwittingly, had camped within a couple of hundred metres of our night stop. Unfortunately, on being discovered, they were off like hares, firing over their shoulders, but they had left behind equipment in their haste.

The follow up continued and, after extricating the Bedford, the remainder of us retired to the police camp at Wedza township and made up for some lost sleep.

On awaking a few hours later I decided, first and foremost, to refuel the truck and, to that end, drove round to the Internal Affairs administration building. It was quite normal to replenish our fuel at any government depot. I walked into the office and approached an elderly clerk working behind the desk. He looked up with disinterest.

"Yes?" he rudely enquired.

I explained my reason for being there and was rather taken aback when he replied

"I can't let you have any fuel."

"Why not?" I queried.

"I need a requisition form because we only have enough allocation to run our own vehicles," came the reply.

"But we always fill up at government depots and this is an emergency."

"Have you run out of fuel?"

"No but..........."

"Then I can't help."

My patience was being severely tried and so, before the altercation got out of hand, I decided to seek help from the Officer in Charge at the police station. He however, was not the slightest bit interested in my problems so I was left with only one solution, an hours drive back to Marandellas, the nearest centre. My escort had disappeared into the labyrinth of beer halls and brothels of the township so, hoping that the follow up troops would not need assistance, I left on my own to search for fuel.

There wasn't a soul to be seen as I drove at breakneck speed down the narrow tarred road until, after what seemed an age, I arrived at Grassland Research Centre on the outskirts of Marandellas. My reception there was the complete opposite to the lack of welcome at Wedza and I was soon on my way back with a full tank. The sun was beginning to dip below the horizon as I negotiated the lonely winding road. Without an escort I felt very vulnerable and the road seemed unending, but eventually the welcome sight of the red roofed police station hove into sight. As I pulled up, a constable came running out of the ops room to tell me that the troop had just radioed in to be collected - my timing had been perfect.

The day was not yet over however. After in-bussing the troop I negotiated my way back to Marandellas and on to the main road to Rusape. I was extremely tired by now and could barely keep my eyes open. It was foolhardy to drive under such conditions, particularly when shouldered with the responsibilities of the wellbeing of my passengers. Somehow I kept going, the troops singing in the back, totally unaware of the state of their driver. Suddenly my whole being was concentrated on a shadowy figure gesticulating with a machete in the middle of the road. With the weight and speed of the truck it would have been suicidal to brake or swerve. I half thought I might be hallucinating again but, as we flashed past with inches to spare, I caught a glimpse of a lone African man staggering backwards.

I stopped in case I had struck him but, although we could not see his body in the darkness, his shouting and swearing from the distance reassured me that he was alive and well, if not a little inebriated.

As a footnote, a few months later, we returned from a late night deployment to find the ops room a hive of activity. We were beckoned in and signalled to keep quiet. The radio sprang into life every few moments and by the excited gibbering, something big was obviously going on. We slowly discerned the fact that the unintelligible shouting was the radio operator at Wedza police station relaying events as the township came under a heavy attack. What we thought was interference was actually the sound of small arms fire, interspersed with heavier explosions of mortars and rockets. The attack carried on for about 2 hours and, fortunately casualties were light, as it turned out that most of the fire was inaccurate, hitting trees and roofs. I couldn't help hoping that the obnoxious INTAF clerk still there. I visualised him cringing in terror beneath his bed. Perhaps he would appreciate what the war was about now and would be a little more co-operative next time.

CHAPTER 17

Mafia

With the worry and stress of closing our business down, the number of call- ups and increased intensity of the war, Vi and I decided that we were in much need of a break. A holiday in Rhodesia was out of the question. No area was free from the threat of terrorism and no roads were safe to drive on after late afternoon. We could have flown to any number of resorts in South Africa but instead we decided that a complete change of climate was required.

September therefore, found us jetting our way to the green and cooler climes of Britain. Vi's mother lived near Newmarket and we spent an idyllic three weeks sampling the soft and gentle life in Suffolk with a tour through the Cotswolds, down to Devon and then back along the South coast, either staying at Bed and Breakfasts or with friends and relatives. All too soon our quiet relaxation ended and we were headed back to Rhodesia.

We had decided to break our journey with a few days in Italy. The reason being to buy a pistol. Guns were expensive in Rhodesia and the situation was such that with me away so often, Vi would be happier having a gun for her personal protection. We had heard that the laws on gun sales were more lax in Italy and had obtained the address of a gun shop in Rome.

We had mentioned our mission to a few friends whilst in England

and we were surprised when on one of our last days, there was a knock on the front door.

On the steps stood a large man who I recognised as having done some building work for my mother-in-law and I remembered that he had a few dubious friends. Although he was big he had a rather shy nature and, shifting uncomfortably from one foot to the other he sheepishly asked, "I heard you were looking for a gun."

"Why, yes" I replied, intrigued by his interest. "A pistol or revolver."

"Oh, I can't get anything that small, but I've got a mate who's got a sub-machine gun for sale if you are interested!"

We landed at Rome late in the evening and took a coach from the airport to the central terminus and a taxi from there to our hotel. The driver got rather excited when I gave him a coin as a tip. After much gesticulating and shouting he eventually left and sometime afterwards, with the help of a calculator, I discovered that the impressive Italian coin was worth about a penny.

We were tired and looking forward to a good nights rest but when we arrived at the hotel we found that the boon of modern civilisation, the computer, had taken it into its head to cancel our booking. The receptionist was very sympathetic and, after profuse apologies he managed to trace a room for us. We were taken up a number of flights of stairs, the fitted carpet disappeared and, after walking up a bare passage, we were shown into a broom closet at the top of the building. With two beds squeezed in there was little room for anything else, but we were too tired to worry. We fitted the kids in top to toe in the one bed and we collapsed into the other.

Our worries were not over yet, because although we were high up in the building, we overlooked a main thoroughfare and, even at that time of the night, the sound of traffic was deafening as the noise was funnelled up from below. I think we managed to catch a couple of hour's of sleep at about 3 a.m., before the city came alive again the next morning. Fortunately, the following day the hotel management found a far better room for us which overlooked a quiet courtyard.

After a continental breakfast we made tracks to the address of the gunsmith. Surprisingly, for a city the size of Rome, we found that by sheer coincidence our hotel was within a block of the street we were looking for. Within minutes we were pushing open the door of a small shop, outside of which hung a large sign displaying the word 'Beretta'.

We were greeted by a swarthy, thickset man dressed in an immaculate pair of blue, casual trousers and a brown, leather jacket, each tailored to show off every contour of his muscular body. Although his chalk white teeth flashed a smile of welcome, his eyes remained cold and emotionless. Such was the power of suggestion that I fleetingly wondered whether he had any Mafia connections.

He spoke in Italian, but quickly changed to excellent English when I introduced myself and stated my business. We were shown a range of small hand guns but the prices were higher than I had expected, then came the sales pitch.

"What you want is a Beretta automatic. There is no finer gun made in the world," and with that he produced a .32 calibre automatic pistol. I had to admit that, as it was primarily for my wife's protection, it was the perfect ladies weapon.

It was small and simple, consisting of only two parts. I enquired about a 9mm or .38 but was told that the .32 was the largest calibre pistol allowed for sale in Italy. We agreed the price and the assistant smiled.

"Could I have your passport please?"

I was a little apprehensive of handing over my passport and, seeing my uncertainty he gave another smile.

"It's just a formality sir. The police have to be certain that you are not resident in Italy."

Having lived for so long with international trade sanctions and the arms embargo against South Africa I was worried about my passport that showed a Rhodesian address. There was nothing for it but to explain my predicament, even if it meant walking out without the gun.

"I'm sure there will be no problem sir," he gushed. "We take the passport and the bill of sale to the police who will issue an export permit and hand back your passport. You will receive the gun at the airport on your departure. OK?"

I had no option and so, still with some doubts, I handed it over. A form had to be filled in and signed and, the next moment, I was back in the street, glancing furtively around and feeling like an international gun runner.

In my naivety I had expected to walk in, buy a gun, and walk out with it but we had been assured that the passport could be picked up two days later, so for the rest of our stay we could be tourists.

Being complete strangers, without a word of Italian between us, we decided that a few organised tours would be better than just walking around. We booked and paid for a trip to see some of the well known Roman Relics and the Catacombes that afternoon and a trip to Capri for the next day. As we had the rest of the morning to kill, we decided to do as the Romans do and took a local bus to the Colosseum.

Using sign language, we found the correct bus which was soon bumping and jolting us through the crowded streets. The entrance to the bus was at the rear where there was an automatic ticket machine in place of a conductor. By watching other passengers I soon realised that one bought a ticket upon entering and then either found a seat or moved down the aisle to eventually exit through the front doors. As we hadn't a clue of how much that fare was or even, for that matter, how to operate the machine, we decided that as all the doors opened at each stop, to remain standing at the rear and just hop off through the incoming doors as soon as we caught sight of our desination. After about half a dozen stops, at each of which we were jostled by the incoming passengers, we did just that and as the bus drew away we congratulated ourselves on getting a free trip.

"Look, ice cream!" called my daughter Sue, pointing to a vendor displaying a mouth-watering variety of ice creams.

Italian ice cream had a reputation which even we knew of in Africa so, as I couldn't resist the temptation, we soon had four large examples picked from the wide choice. I held two while Vi went to take her purse from her handbag. I took a lick and the delicious taste and texture slid smoothly down my throat. It was gorgeous, with a taste so different to the ice cream that we were used to at home.

"My purse has gone!" cried out Vi.

The ice hit my stomach like sour cream.

"Are you sure?" I enquired lamely. "Have you looked properly?"

"Of course," she snapped back, tears welling up in her eyes, "It had all our money in it."

My legs felt weak and I sat down on a nearby step. I was shattered. All our money gone, a strange city in a foreign country, a language we didn't know and two young children to look after and two days before our flight left. I felt so helpless, I could have cried.

A pickpocket must have lifted the purse on the bus. Our free ride had suddenly become very expensive.

I had just enough change to pay for the ice creams and we headed back to the hotel. The Colosseum no longer held any attraction. It was just an old ruin in a hostile city.

With no money, we started the long trudge back and Vi and I discussed our problem as we walked. By now we had calmed down and remembered that we still had some traveller's cheques hidden in our room. We had only lost the money cashed at the bank that morning.

Feeling slightly relieved, the walk seemed a little easier, despite having to carry two very tired children. Back in our room we reassessed our financial position. Something we had both forgotten was the fact that we had paid for the hotel in advance and also our tours. The money we still had was to pay for the pistol whilst that which had been stolen was our spending money for the rest of our stay. The situation was looking a little better but could we still afford the pistol and survive two more days?

After careful calculations we decided to go with the pistol. That was the only reason we were in Rome and we were determined not to be beaten. It would mean that we would have to be very thrifty and eke out our last few liras.

At breakfast, when the waiter's backs were turned, we would surreptitiously filch rolls, packs of butter and jam. Secreted in Vi's handbag, they would stave of the pangs of hunger during the day.

We started to relax and enjoyed our tours that, on the trip to Capri included lunch and dinner. Our main problem was the number of shops and stalls to which the tour guide kept steering us. Even at lunch we had the embarrassment of two young men, one with an accordion and the other singing, serenading us and then demanding a tip, with which we were unfortunately, unable to oblige. Towards the end of the tour we had a nagging feeling that our guide had all his friends and relations in on the act.

We survived the ordeal however, and at last it was time to pay our last visit to the gun shop. We were relieved to hear that our export licence had been granted and I gratefully pocketed my passport. We then received our instructions from the salesman. He pointed to another mafioso lurking in the dim recesses behind him.

"Mario will meet you at the coach station. He will be wearing a black coat and trilby hat. What will you be wearing?"

I was tempted to say a carnation in my buttonhole but, by his humourless countenance, it may not have gone down very well. I described my corduroy jeans and shirt but pointed out that my tall stature shouldn't be too hard to spot in a crowd. I handed over the precious liras we had saved, hoping that Mario would indeed be there and that this was not a con trick.

Later that day we took a taxi back to the coach station and, with our funds perilously low, left another irate taxi driver with a worthless tip and carried our bags inside the terminal. We found the airport coach and soon espied Mario, not only wearing his trench coat and trilby hat, but sporting black leather gloves and carrying a package under his arm. I went to greet him but was turned away with a fierce shake of his head and, without a word, he indicated that we should board the coach. Feeling as though we were taking part in a cloak and dagger drama, we took our seats and Mario slipped into a place a few rows behind us.

On arriving at the airport, Mario's tactics changed completely. Rushing over to us he took hold of my arm and muttered 'Polizia' I looked around, wondering in a panic what he was talking about. Was he about to shop us in for gun running? With no option, he led me firmly over to a side room where a policeman in uniform was ensconced behind a desk. He looked up without interest as we entered, and waved me to sit down. Taking the package from Mario, he opened it and laid the pistol on the table.

"Passport," he snapped.

Meekly I handed it over and he carefully checked the details.

"Come this way."

I could already feel the cold steel of the handcuffs closing over my wrists. Sweat trickled down my neck. We marched over to a counter where I recognised our luggage.

"Open this case." he commanded.

Apprehensively, I complied and he thrust the package into the case, at the same time jabbering something to the Italian customs officers. The cases were removed and he turned and handed back my passport,

"Just report to emigration over there," and with a smile. "I hope you have enjoyed your stay in Italy."

Then he was gone. Of Mario there was no sign.

Shortly afterwards, as the plane took off, we sank back thankfully in our seats, glad to see the Italian landscape slipping away beneath us.

CHAPTER 18

Spine Chillers

By 1977 every facet of life was being affected by the war. Each radio or television news bulletin would start with a security force bulletin and the statement one dreaded to hear was 'Security Force Headquarters regret to announce …………' followed by the names of those persons, black or white, civilian or army, who had been killed or injured in a farm attack, landmine explosion or some similar incident.

By now all able bodied white men were on a call up rota of some sort. Even those of very dubious medical categories had been found jobs, albeit in town or close to cities on clerical or transport duties.

Our social life was disrupted as well as our business lives, but when we were home from the bush there was a never ending social whirl. It was too dangerous to leave the city limits after dark and, I suppose, looking back, one took comfort from each other being together in a crisis.

A strange phenomenon was to be seen at the cinemas and theatres where the audiences were mainly women, usually in groups keeping each other company, their respective husbands and boyfriends being away.

A number of marriages couldn't take the strain of the daily upheaval and lonely wives would fall prey to the advances of a neighbouring male friend, who might be in town, while the husband was away. One heard the occasional tale of a philandering husband using the call up system to his own advantage by taking the opportunity of holidaying with a girlfriend while his wife worried, believing that he was in danger on call up.

In the city, camouflage uniforms were to be seen everywhere and strange looking army vehicles, with mine protected bodywork, scurried about. At work, it was not at all unusual, for a customer leaving a car for repair, to hand over a rifle or pistol to be locked away until their return.

Vi and I always carried our pistol with us whenever we went out at night, but an incident at Christmas taught us to carry it at all times. We found that we had a quiet day over the holiday period and so we decided to take the kids out to Lake McIlwaine which was about 25 kilometres south-west of the city. The huge earth dam wall, reputed to be the largest in the southern hemisphere, at Hunyani Poort, was always impressive when, in the rainy season, the lake swelled to bursting point, and the water roared down the spillway.

On the drive out there, Vi asked if we should have brought the pistol with us. It hadn't occurred to me, as it was mid morning, and the danger period was twilight or darkness.

We had gone too far to turn back and as there were a few other vehicles on the road, we carried on. Turning off the main road onto the short dirt access road I pulled up in the deserted car park; the nearby cafe was closed and boarded up. The silence pervading the valley was broken only by the distant rumble of the water pounding down the spillway. Feeling slightly uneasy, we walked to the top of the wall. A mild breeze cooled us from the open water, the wall vibrated beneath our feet as the flood curled over the edge of the spillway and hurtled into the gap between the hills. Vi nudged me to point out two Africans walking through the car park below. Nervously we watched them climb the narrow path towards us but on reaching our level they appeared to be sightseers like ourselves.

Still feeling uneasy, we decided to call it a day and made our way back to the car. With our nerves on edge, and the children firmly sandwiched between us, it was difficult not to run. As soon as we reached the main road we relaxed and joked about being so silly to have felt scared.

Two days later, within half a mile of the dam wall, a farmers wife and her daughter were gunned down after returning home from a shopping trip at midday.

*

It is inevitable that, when being actively involved at the front line of a war, incidents will be witnessed so far removed from civilian life that, looking back on them years later, they seem like a dream. Was I actually there?

One morning, after stand-to, we heard the sound of helicopters. Wave after wave of Allouettes throbbed overheard like dragonflies. This was obviously more than Fire Force out on a spree. To get a better view we drove up the hill to the radio tower, from which we gained a comprehensive view over the surrounding countryside. Through binoculars, the air field at Rusape could just be distinguished and it was alive with helicopters. As they took off they were joined in the sky by Hawker Hunter jet fighters and Canberra bombers. They were all heading for the Mozambique border and we knew that we were witnessing something really big. We didn't know at that stage that we were watching the build-up of what was to be one of the largest strikes by our armed forces on a terrorist base camp over the border.

I watched the invasion force with mixed feelings. On the one hand I was awed by the sight of so much power and hoped that the raid would be a success. On the other hand I couldn't help feeling a tinge of sorrow for those young lives which would end that day.

As a transport driver I was never involved in the questioning of villagers and suspects, but I had become aware that items such as a bucket of water or a cattle probe were used to speed up the process. At the same time I realised that one had to be rather naive to think that in any war, when lives are at stake, the side you are on is going to fight strictly to the Marquis of Queensbury's rules. Even so, it was hard to feel comfortable with oneself when witnessing a local being roughed up and humiliated to obtain information. Some of the worst excesses, surprisingly, were African against African.

One such incident occurred when an African Sergeant Major was driving a vehicle behind me. I had passed a lone African man walking beside the road and thought nothing of it. The Sergeant however, had other ideas. Probably being frustrated at the lack of action, he decided to search and question the walker. Amongst his possessions the man had a letter written to a friend abhorring the war situation. I thought it was quite innocent but the Sergeant insisted on further questioning of the man. It went a bit further than questioning however and when things started to get violent I had to step in to stop it. The Sergeant was livid at my interference, but I insisted that if the man was to be questioned at all, it should be by the proper authorities. We therefore took him with us to the police station at Rusape and we heard later that he was quite innocent. The whole incident was totally unnecessary but, because of his disgusting treatment at the hands of the security forces, this man would probably henceforth sympathise with the terrorists.

Another incident that was very unsettling, not just for me, but also for the other drivers present, was when we parked with a full troop near a country store to await instructions. We suddenly realised that a number of the store's goods were appearing on the back of the trucks. Unbeknown to us, the store keeper was being kept occupied at the counter while the goods were being lifted out of the back door as fast as they could go.

This was straightforward looting of an innocent shop keeper. We registered our disquiet with the troop commanders, who showed no interest in our concern, so the only way we drivers could stop it was to insist on moving the convoy further away.

What upset us most about this incident though, was that the troop commanders were not prepared to take disciplinary action and it was left to us drivers to report the incident to the relevant authorities. Even then we were never sure if any subsequent action was taken.

*

Some incidents were of a macabre and horrific nature. Some we could joke about, but some were more serious.

Bill was in his fifties, a family man with a very easy going personality, the sort of person who made friends easily and was himself very popular. Strangely though, he seemed to be fascinated by death. Whenever a driver was needed to pick up equipment and bodies after a contact, Bill would be the first to volunteer.

One day an escort was required by the local police to go to a village where there was a suicide victim. Bill was up and gone before we knew what had happened. Later, as we were having our lunch, he returned and cheerfully regaled us with the details of the corpse.

On one occasion we arrived at Inyazura police station to pick up a troop. Standing in the yard was a Land Rover around which a small crowd had gathered. In the back, surrounded by arms and equipment, were two bodies. At that moment, a Police Inspector lead out a scruffy and scared looking young African who was probably no more than a teenager.

"Come and meet your mates."

The youngster looked ready to faint.

"Is this your mate?" the Inspector pointed at one body, "Perhaps you'd recognise him better this way," and with that he heaved one of the cadavers into a sitting position and, with his hand, moved it about like a ventriloquists dummy. The large white eyes rolled and rocked from behind the death mask. The terrorist suspect had to be supported as he swayed at the knees.

It was an unpleasant incident that fortunately was rare but showed how brutalised some people became under the tension and worry of a war situation.

*

Whilst relaxing in front of our quarters one day a call came in for an escort to accompany the local police into the Makoni Tribal Trust Land. A villager had reported a body lying on open ground. Barry duly set off with four troopies in a Hyena and what was to follow was one of those peculiar runs of coincidence that make a war strange and impossible to comprehend.

The location of the body was a bit vague and the villager who had reported it wasn't too sure which one of the maze of trails would lead to the spot. After meandering down a number of different tracks the guide thought he recognised a rocky outcrop with a clump of aloes growing on the side of a hill. Everyone debussed and commenced searching for the body. After a fruitless search they regrouped to discuss their next move and, while doing so, they became aware of a disturbance nearby. Over a ridge two figures appeared wielding rifles and roughly pushing an old man before them. As the search party dived for cover the terrorists opened fire and ran, leaving their bewildered prisoner in the cross fire. The ters soon disappeared and the police radioed for assistance to commence a follow up.

The first I knew of this was when I was called to bus Whiskey troop into the area. Barry could give no exact location so it was our turn to wander around the network of sandy tracks.

At one stage we stopped and the troops debussed to search on foot because we knew we were getting close by the strength of the radio signal. We eventually discovered we were on opposite sides of a valley and, after studying the maps, we worked out a route.

By now the terrorists had vanished and the villages and fields were deserted. The local population always went to ground when trouble appeared.

Whiskey troop moved out in search of the ters and I joined Barry's contingent in the search for the missing body. Eventually we spotted it on sloping ground just a short distance from a small group of African mud huts. We parked and walked over to the grotesque sight.

The body was of a young women lying face down and was barely recognisable from dismemberment by animals and the general bloating brought about from days in the open bush under the sun. Despite the condition of the remains however it was quite evident how she had died. At least fifty bullet holes were still visible. It was sickening to think of what had happened to this poor girl. Had she been accused of being an informer? Possibly refused to give favours to the terrorists or had she been killed as an example to the locals to toe the line? We would never know. Whatever had happened, it had been quite deliberate and carried out in cold blood. An AK47 magazine takes thirty rounds so either there were two executioners or one who had reloaded in the middle of the act.

We made our way to what we thought were deserted huts but found a woman trying to hide. She was pregnant and very frightened. She refused to come into the open as, under African custom, if a pregnant woman lays eyes on a dead person then she will lose her unborn child. When questioned she replied that the terrorists had killed the girl as a reprisal and that they had threatened the villagers with more deaths if the body was buried. It was to stay in the open as a terrible reminder.

We couldn't leave things like that so, before we left, arrangements were made to bury the body.

An interesting tailpiece to this episode came from Whiskey troop a few days later. While they were tracking the two terrorists seen earlier, darkness fell and they made camp in the scrub. Later that night they were woken with a start by a shout nearby.

"One"

"Two," came a shout a little way off.

"Three," from a further distance.

"Four," faintly.

Throughout the night this numbering off came at regular intervals. As daylight filtered through the trees the troops realised that they had accidentally bedded down close to a terrorist encampment with the guards checking on each other by number. As the light became clearer the full extent of the opposition could be assessed. They had stumbled upon a large meeting of various groups of terrorists and they were outnumbered by about five to one. Fire force was alerted immediately but, because the powers that be thought that Whiskey troop were exaggerating, by the time they eventually appeared most of the groups had disappeared. Even so contact was made and a number of terrorists killed. Ironically if the terrorists hadn't insisted on the girls body being left in the open our troops wouldn't have been in the area.

CHAPTER 19

The Wrong Drop Off Point at the Right Time

The day started as a routine deployment. A number of 'sticks' were to be dropped off at various points from where a sweep of the area would be carried out whilst a hidden O.P., established in the hills a few days earlier, would observe if any untoward movement of locals appeared.

All was going well and I had just one stick left to drop off led by an African Sergeant Major. Bill was escorting me in the Hyena and, as soon as we left the influence of the troop commander, the Sgt. Major stood up overlooking the cab of the Puma, binoculars around his neck, directing operations as if he was Rommel in the desert. I wasn't impressed by his antics as I knew exactly where he was to be deployed and, until he left the vehicle, I was in charge. We were in an area I knew well and, as we lumbered past the St Triashill mission buildings and down the track onto an open grassy plateau, I could see movement on the scrub covered hills above a small village. As we got closer I could see a number of young men running up the slopes and, by coincidence, the drop off point was beside the group of mud huts. As we approached the spot it became obvious that the men were fleeing from us. I had never witnessed this sort of behaviour before by villagers and assumed that they must be guilty of some misdemeanour, or perhaps they had had experience of some of our more enthusiastic troops. As we stopped in a cloud of dust I yelled. "Debus," but there was no response.

"Wrong place," sneered the Sgt arrogantly.

"It is not the wrong place," I replied heatedly. "If you hurry you could catch those men."

"That's no matter," he replied dismissively. "Go on further."

I was surprised at his disinterest but as there was, in fact, a point further on that would cut off part of a corner, I decided that it was pointless to argue and carried on for the short distance. As I got there."Go further on," came the command from behind.

He wasn't interested in the absconders or in starting his sweep from the correct place. After some argument, I radioed 151Alpha for advice. Unfortunately Fred Mason, the C.O., wasn't available. The radio operator was nonplussed, and could offer no assistance, so eventually we reached a compromise. I would take the Sergeant wherever he wanted and then radio his new position back to them, from where he would start his sweep. I realised, as we trundled further on however, that he was trying to cut out two hills and a valley from his patrol's walk. The track was deteriorating badly by now and, as we climbed over a ridge, the bottom of the truck scraped over granite boulders. I stopped, and this time the Sergeant realised that I was going no further.

"This will do fine," he stated, not wanting to lose face.

Before he and his stick disappeared on patrol, I made sure that they helped turn the Puma round, which took quite a lot of pushing and shoving as the wheels jammed between the rocks. Bill in the Hyena was almost facing in the right direction when there was a loud crack and a clatter. The prop shaft had broken. My patience, by now was sorely tried, and the Sergeant decided to depart as quickly as possible. I couldn't help feeling that if he had debussed at the correct place, we would be happily driving back to camp as it was, we had no tools and no towing equipment.

I radioed our position and our plight back to base. They arranged for another vehicle to bring a chain and my instructions were to make my way back past the mission to the main road to collect it. Our escort was meagre. Bill and one constable stayed with the hyena while the other constable came with me. As it happened I need not have worried because the run back to the main road was uneventful. We collected the tow chain and set off on the return trip but we hadn't gone far when the radio crackled into life. I couldn't believe my ears when I heard the errant Sergeant calling excitedly that he had spotted ters in the open and wanted 'Fire Force' immediately. By the time that we had got back to the mission, which was about half way to the stricken Hyena, a Dakota could be seen circling overhead. 'Fire Force' had arrived. At that moment 151 Alpha called me to proceed to a location somewhere between the mission and Bill to await an incoming helicopter.

As we waited, my thoughts went back to that light hearted lecture at the hard square, with the wooden chair helicopter, which now seemed so long ago. I idly wondered what we were picking up: troops? arms? We didn't have long to wait to find out. As I had parked on high ground with the contact going on in the valley below, I had no warning of the arrival of the chopper until it suddenly popped over the rim of the plateau and homed in on us, flying a few feet above the ground like a demented bee.

After it had touched down I awaited the thumbs up from the pilot before the constable and I ran at a crouch to the side opening. There on the floor of the chopper lay the body of a dead terrorist. It wasn't quite what I had expected but, recovering my composure quickly, we carried the body back to the truck. Wasting no time, the chopper lifted off to return to the foray, leaving us the task of lifting the body into the back of the truck.

It was now that I learned the full meaning of the expression 'dead weight'. The floor of the Puma was well over a metre from the ground so the constable climbed up to take the body as I lifted it. The ter was dressed in their normal uniform of blue denim jeans and jacket. His midrift was stained dark red where a burst of cannon fire had caught him across his right thigh and pelvis. The sightless eyes and mouth set in a deathly smirk disturbed me slightly but, nevertheless, I grasped him under the armpits and heaved him up. He must have weighed about 80kgs and, after a considerable amount of effort, I managed to pull him upright. As I did so, he emitted a loud belch! In the shock I nearly dropped him. My strength was ebbing fast as I heaved again, only this time to find his head lolled forward beneath the step of the floor. At the third attempt, and after much heaving and pushing, we somehow managed to get him up on the floor.

All this time we had been in open ground so, while we waited for the battle to end, we parked up under the cover of some trees until the all clear came over the radio.

Back at the Hyena it didn't take long to hitch up the chain and, cautiously, we started to retrace our steps. Our main worry was that if any stragglers from the contact were coming our way, we would be vulnerable to an ambush. We hadn't travelled far when, rounding a corner, I found a tree trunk partially blocking the road. It certainly had not been there on the way up and so, with heart thumping and eyes peeled for trouble, I squeezed the Puma through the gap, but only silence answered us. Minutes later, my forehead was suddenly covered with beads of sweat as it dawned on me that we had been extremely lucky that there hadn't been a land mine planted in that gap.

As we slowly trundled back to 151 Alpha I couldn't help reflecting on the incredible luck that the Sergeant had had. If he had debussed at the correct location it would have been extremely unlikely that he would have spotted the terrorists. It was a matter of being in the wrong place at the right time.

A consequence of that day was to affect me a few days later. While we had been waiting in the bush for clearance to rescue the Hyena I had caught a finger on a razor sharp piece of grass. Within 48 hours it had swelled up with infection, to such a degree that I asked permission to attend the small hospital in Rusape to get it lanced. Superintendent Mason was most indignant, "Certainly not," he retorted. "Get one of the medics in the camp to sort it out."

Each stick had one member trained in basic first aid, there was only one troop in camp at that time and I was rather taken aback when I found the only qualified person available was a tall, very muscular African Sergeant. The last time I had seen him was a few days previously, fearsomely striding out from the bush, toting a machine gun with bandoleers of ammunition slung over his shoulders after a contact.

He took one look at the swelling, fetched his medical kit and took hold of my hand. Apprehensively I looked away and waited for the pain of the incision. A moment later he was bandaging my finger up.

"Is that it?" I gasped.

The soldier nodded; I hadn't felt a thing from this gentle giant.

*

Occasionally some strange contact with the terrorists would occur. Sometimes a letter would turn up at the base camp, usually addressed to the C.O., from a terrorist leader. Generally it would be of a threatening nature and, what was unnerving, was that various members of the security forces would be named and occasionally even nicknames were used, but fortunately they never mentioned the 'tall driver', otherwise I would have been off like a shot.

Their intelligence was usually surprisingly good, which proved that there were enemy 'eyes' within the camp, but we never found out who it was.

During one contact, while exchanging fire, the ters had taken cover behind some rocks on a small kopje, pinning down our troops behind a country store. One of our troopies had distinctive fair hair and, during a lull in the fighting and in the silence, a voice could be heard calling. "Just give us the blond one, and you can all go free."

"'Oh, we like the blond one."

"Give us the blond one."

By this time, as you can imagine, 'the blond one's' nerves were shattered. Fortunately, before anything else could happen, a relief troop arrived and the tables were turned. After that incident however, 'blondie' was never too keen to go out on patrol.

*

Not far from 151 Alpha was, what was referred to as, the 'Gook Farm' The word 'Gook' being borrowed from the American forces in Vietnam. As drivers, and not privy to some of the goings on behind the scenes, we discovered the 'Gook Farm' accidentally when Ben had to call there to pick 'someone' up and bring him back to camp.

Ben had expected a civilian to greet him and was most surprised when he met someone in camouflage kit. It was quite evident, from the various vehicles and equipment around the place, that this was a security force camp of some sort.

The person he had to collect was known as a Majiba or Tiger. He, or sometimes she, was a terrorist or terrorist sympathiser who had been persuaded to change sides. They were basically informers who we hoped would lead us to terrorist groups or arms caches and sometimes the farm went one stage further, with the more trustworthy being retrained and equipped with FN rifles and our normal equipment. Who better to know the terrorist ways than the terrorist himself?

It didn't always work however, and occasionally we were led on a wild goose chase looking for arms or ters. In one incident I recall a Majiba, who was so petrified of betraying his companions, that he shot himself in the foot by accident sic prior to our embarkation.

*

The majority of deployments would normally go like clockwork. We would drive to the drop off point, deploy the troops and then return to the base camp.

Although this would usually be at night on narrow bush roads, if one considered the number of trips we made, we were often tucked up snugly in bed by the small hours of the morning, satisfied that the job had gone well.

There were exceptions however, and one of those was a total disaster. We had deployed into the Chiduku so many times that we were surprised, at the briefing, to be given a location in an area with which we were unfamiliar.

Following the directions from our maps we turned the two Pumas right at a T junction onto, what should have been, the correct road, but the surface soon started to deteriorate badly and it didn't look as though there had been any traffic for some time. Eventually we had to slowly ease the vehicles over deep ruts and exposed boulders. According to the map there was a river ahead and I approached the crossing with trepidation. My caution was well founded because, instead of a gentle slope into a ford or a bridge, the track petered out at the crumbling banks of the river. The headlight beams, that had been playing on the dusty track and scrub, suddenly disappeared into a black void. I braked and clambered down from the cab and, with the help of a strong torch, could just make out the reflection of dark water a metre or so below the bank. The torch beam wasn't bright enough to make out the opposite bank. Obviously there was no chance of crossing here.

We now had the problem of turning the Pumas round. The track was very narrow and, as we tried to turn the first truck, it stuck fast in the muddy ruts. After much pushing and shoving it finally came free and, by the time we had managed to turn the second truck around, there was scarcely a man not covered in mud. There was a lot of muttering about incompetent drivers taking the wrong road but in fact our maps were not up to date and, on retracing our steps, we found that the junction had been moved half a kilometre to enable a safer river crossing.

By now we were several hours late, tired and dirty so we were relieved when we eventually found the correct drop off point and could head for home. The return trip was uneventful as far as Rusape, although, as we lurched our way over the rough road skirting Lake Lesapi, I was conscious of a lot of radio activity. It was always a problem deciphering radio messages whilst bouncing over potholes and corrugations so, as we gained the quiet of the smooth tarred road, on the outskirts of the town, I was apprehensive as I heard the dreaded call. "Mantle Mobile One this is 151Alpha, are you reading us? Come in Mobile One."

"151Alpha, this is Mobile ...."

"Where the hell have you been?" cut in Fred Masons voice harshly. Before I could reply, he ordered. "Get back to the drop off point. There's been an accident. One man is severely injured. Get back as quickly as you can."

My heart sank as I thought of the distance we had to go back over the unmade roads into the Chiduku. As time was of the essence, all thoughts of land mines and ambushes were forgotten as we raced back down the narrow twisting tracks, past sleeping villages, until we arrived back to see a figure step out from the shadows. It was the troop leader. I switched off and clambered out of the cab. I became aware that the rest of the troop was spread around in the moonlight. The only sound was the quiet sobbing of grieving comrades.

It transpired that, within minutes of the troop moving off in formation from the drop off point, a shot rang out. Thinking that they had walked into an ambush, they flung themselves on the ground, but when all remained quiet they regrouped, only to find that one of the sergeants was missing. When they eventually located his prostrate form they found that he had been hit by one shot to the head which had removed part of his skull and brain.

We loaded the body onto the truck and the troop started to climb aboard to return to camp. This was not to be however. Fred Mason was adamant that the exercise must carry on and, despite vociferous protests from the inspector in charge of the troop, they eventually completed their five day patrol.

Whether the decision to keep the patrol out was correct, I was not in a position to judge, but to have heard hardened soldiers crying for their comrade and seen morale reduced to such a low ebb, it was difficult to see any good coming from the enforced five day patrol. Their minds would have been in shock, as they dwelt on the horror of the incident, instead of concentrating on the job in hand.

The subsequent inquiry proved that the shot had come from an FN rifle carried by a member of his own troop. The sergeant had been a well liked and respected member of the troop and the incident was recorded as an accidental discharge. Having seen the misery this caused I began to appreciate the fury with which the troopie had been punished at the battle camp some months previously.

CHAPTER 20

One-Five-One-Charlie

As a general rule, three drivers were called up every two weeks for deployment to the Rusape district. Two would be based at 151 Alpha, which was a large camp employing four or five troops; each retained there for six week tours of duty. On the far eastern side of the Chiduku, in the Wedza TTL, was located the 151Charlie camp. This was a small camp, with only one troop and, from the stories we had heard, rather primitive. Consequently, we would do anything to stay in the relative comforts of 151 Alpha, and try not to draw the short straw for 151 Charlie.

One morning I arrived at Tomlinson Depot, at the start of another two-week stint, to be greeted by two of my Bulawayo booze cruise companions. As they always paired up on call ups (as did Barry and I) I realised that this time I had, at last, drawn the short straw.

I met Inspector Nobby Clark, the commander of Romeo Troop stationed at 151Charlie, and was soon following him into the wilds of the Chiduku. We travelling far deeper into that part of the country than I had been before and, just before dusk, I spied, through the dusty bush, the national flag flying from a post in the middle of a small, but neatly laid out, camp.

At the entrance a gaily painted sign welcomed us to the local beer hall that was now the basis of 151Charlie. The original mud brick buildings, with corrugated iron roofs, were still standing in the centre of the camp. The ops room and radio equipment occupied the store room whilst the main building, the door of which still proclaimed in faded paint that it was the 'Bar Lounge', was used as the mess and kitchen. The veranda was piled with equipment, deep freezers and generators. Faded adverts for Lion and Castle beer enticed us from the walls although, paradoxically, the camp was 'dry', with cool drinks and coffee being the order of the day.

The remainder of the camp was reminiscent of a scene from the Boer War, with neat rows of canvas tents lining each side of a square. Sandbagged trenches offered some protection if attacked and the perimeter was fenced with rolls of barbed wire and criss-crossed with a complex system of trip wires.

The ablution facilities consisted of a lean-to constructed of poles and hessian at one end of the main building, acting as a bathroom, with the original beer hall toilets a short walk outside the fence.

The bathroom consisted of a couple of hand basins with mirrors, filched from the lounge, still covered with beer adverts but, taking pride of place in the middle of the floor, was the bath. This was no ordinary bath though. Purpose built in bricks and plaster, measuring well over two metres long and a metre wide, this gargantuan white painted vessel had to be the luxury to end all luxuries in this forgotten piece of Africa. Over the next two weeks I was to spend many pleasant hours soaking my dusty frame in this mini swimming pool.

The water to fill this edifice was drawn from what was known as a 'Rhodesian Boiler'. This consisted of an old 200 litre oil drum, fed from a local water supply, suspended on a brick or iron frame over a wood fire. They were very efficient at providing boiling water, if the fire was well stoked, and were used throughout the more primitive country districts.

Our only source of water, other than for drinking purposes, was a small dam close by. The water, like all waterways in Rhodesia was infested with the Bilharzia snail and any contact could result in a most unpleasant disease where microscopic organisms could attack various organs in ones body, such as the liver, kidneys or the brain. A cure was available, if caught early, so everyone had to have regular checks at the police hospital and luckily I never caught the illness. The boiling water must have killed off the germs.

The toilets at 151 Charlie were to block up within a couple of days of my arrival and, although a basic 'long drop' was dug a few metres from the camp, most of us opted to try to wait until we were in more civilised surroundings. This meant that if, on one of our excursions, we were near an INTAF fort, police station or mining village there was a stampede for the toilet, almost before the vehicle had stopped. Being the driver, this usually meant that I was last in line.

Other than the disastrous toilet facilities, the camp was comfortable, the gas operated deep freezers keeping our meat and vegetables fresh, and we enjoyed many a good meal in the 'bar lounge'.

Romeo Troop was unfortunate in having seen virtually no action during the war and morale was low. The troop commander had been charged to try to improve the situation but to no avail. Morale was so low that, a few weeks before this posting, one of the young conscripts had 'borrowed' a Land Rover and driven home to be AWOL for a few days. Although he was now back on duty, he was awaiting the outcome of his court martial. This did nothing to relieve the general gloom which pervaded the camp.

Nobby Clark, the troop commander, was a very honest and religious man who, although I got on well with him, was too upright and equitable to be successful in this type of war. I had sufficient experience by now to know that the successful troops tended to be less scrupulous and bent the rules to suit the occasion. They were generally tougher and harder of character and didn't mind ruffling a few feathers to get a result.

Romeo Troop had only a few days left of their tour of duty and my time was occupied in bringing in patrols from the surrounding area. It all appeared to be quiet, the only event of interest was when the spare wheel fell off the back of my Puma as I was fording a stream. The tyre, being filled with water for mine protection, must have weighed about 100 kg, and it took the combined efforts of my escort and me to lift it back onto its cradle. We threw caution to the wind and laid down our arms to do this but as we were surrounded by granite kopjes, which made for an ideal ambush position, we were relieved that all remained quiet.

That night, because of being such a small camp, I was roped in for guard duty. The night was divided into one hour shifts and I was on from 10 p.m. to 11 p.m. An hour is an awfully long time when you are alone at night while everyone else sleeps. Every so often I would stroll near the perimeter fence and as I peered out into the veldt the moonlight seemed to distort every tree and rock until I was convinced that someone was out there.

At the end of my stint I handed over to the next guard, who happened to be the radio operator. He was fast asleep in the radio room and, when I tried to wake him, it was as if he was drugged. Eventually I managed to haul him to his feet and I left him standing there blinking in the light. I was awoken by an exasperated Nobby in the early morning.

"Did you hand over to the next guard last night?"

I affirmed that I had and explained how difficult it had been to wake my successor. It appeared that he had fallen back to sleep so the whole camp had slept peacefully through half the night, blissfully unaware that we had no guard. If the enemy had known that, they could have ignored all our defences and simply walked through the main entrance.

I remembered the tale of a previous driver on guard duty at the same camp some months earlier who, startled by a noise and some movement, had opened fire with his FN, arousing the camp to battle stations. After some minutes the troop commander, realising that there was no return of fire, ordered his men to cease firing. All remained on the alert in the trenches until morning. In the cold light of day they discovered the cause of the alarm. A goat, who had been caught in the maze of trip wires, was nonchalantly munching what grass was within its reach with not a scratch from the hail of bullets during the skirmish.

Whiskey troop arrived to take over a few days later and for one night we had two troops squeezed into the meagre accommodation. Everything changed with the arrival of Whiskey Troop. They were having a very successful war, with one of the highest 'kill' rates in Support Unit. One immediately sensed that these were harder, no nonsense veterans. Morale was high and they were here to do a job.

All base camps were supposed to be dry, so I was surprised that evening, to see beer crates being brought into the mess. Soon the beer was flowing and, between the games of cards and the songs, a disapproving Nobby retired to his tent in disgust.

The troop was noisy and boisterous and, on reflection, it struck me that the raised voices, booming out throughout the night air, were issuing a challenge to anyone within earshot and onto the bush telegraph that a new troop had arrived - so beware.

Nobby had words about the frivolity with Inspector John Armitage, the commander of Whiskey Troop, the next morning but John made it quite clear that he was in charge from now on and would do things his way. I felt sorry for Nobby because he was a very decent man who had been well trained and did everything by the book, but was like a duck out of water in this situation.

The trucks were loaded in preparation for Romeo Troop's departure and soon the trek was on, under the protection of a Whiskey Troop escort as far as Wedza, where the roads were fully tarred and relatively safe from there onwards. With heavily laden vehicles the going was slow. Each troop was fully equipped and self contained for its six week tour, even to carrying with them their own deep freezers.

Half way to Wedza we had to negotiate a pass that meandered between some low hills. In the normal way, with the convoy well spaced out and plenty of escort vehicles, we would have driven straight through, but Nobby insisted on his troop carrying out a wide sweep ahead on foot. Naturally this slowed us even more and it was with great relief that, after hours of dusty travel, we came into sight of the red corrugated iron roofs of the Wedza settlement. Our return to camp was considerably quicker with Whiskey Troop ignoring such precautions.

The next night we started deploying to areas that John Armitage had decided might be worth looking at and I dropped off two sticks, who would operate O.Ps., near a mission. Although, in my experience, no mission centre had ever proved to be subversive, the terrorists had a reputation for staying close by and using them as safe houses.

The next afternoon I retraced my steps to Wedza with just one stick, whereupon a strange episode took place. I had thought that this was to be just another deployment so, when we arrived at the police camp, I was surprised to be included in the full briefing.

The briefing was carried out behind locked doors and shuttered windows by a Special Branch Inspector. Three Whiskey Troop members donned terrorist style denim trousers and jackets and AK 47 assault rifles were exchanged for their FN's. Various other ter paraphernalia was slung around them until, to all intents and purposes, three terrorists stood before us. Our orders were to accompany the three pseudo ters to a spot about one hours walk from a village suspected of being sympathetic to the terrorist cause. I, with an escort, would stay close to the truck whilst our three friends would walk quite openly into the suspect village.

Meanwhile the rest of the stick would keep the village under observation in case of trouble. There was a risk that there could already be terrorists in this village who might be suspicious of our pseudo ters . Whatever ensued depended on the success of the mission. I discovered some while afterwards that this type of clandestine work was strictly prohibited except to the very specialised units like the Selous Scouts and the SAS, but the Special Branch officer had the reputation of being a bit of a maverick.

Deployment was to be at midnight so we returned to the mess to try to get some sleep. The operation would take the whole night and, with luck, we would be back in Wedza for breakfast. I slept fitfully until I was roused close to midnight. A cup of hot coffee restored my faculties and, on arriving at the Puma, dark figures could be seen huddled in the back, talking in whispers. It was a clear night with a full moon bathing the countryside in its ghostly glow. After about ten kilometres I extinguished the lights to drive the last part by moonlight, a tap on my shoulder signalled the dispersal point. Unfortunately we were in open ground and there was no cover close to the road, so we abandoned the Puma and left it standing like a stranded whale on a moonlit beach.

As the pseudo ters and the troopies disappeared up a nearby track, so the remainder of us dispersed into what cover we could find. The truck was too dangerous to stay with as it was a large and obvious target. I crawled under a line of trees in deep shadow and soon there was silence.

I closed my eyes but sleep would not come and unfortunately there was a good three or four hours to wait.

After about an hour I was startled into alertness by the crackling of twigs nearby. My heart pounded as I peered from my hiding place, rifle at the ready. A dark form loomed up and, with great relief, I recognised the shape of a cow as it lumbered past. It appeared to be blind or drunk as it struggled through the undergrowth and lumbered towards a clump of bushes where some of the escort were concealed. There were muffled cries of indignation when it eventually stumbled upon them. Still unperturbed, the cow carried on towards some nearby huts, destroying a fence surrounding some crops until it eventually dislodged a chicken house from its pedestal. With indignant clucking, the chickens spilt out in disarray and eventually the cow disappeared into the obscurity of bushes and trees in the distance. There were no enquiring sounds or movement from the huts and soon silence descended again.

A pre-arranged signal had been arranged so that we wouldn't accidentally open fire on our returning troops but, after a few more hours of uncomfortable intermittent dozing, I suddenly became aware of dark forms creeping up the road and grouping near the Puma. Feeling sure that they were our troops I thankfully crept from my hiding place and stretched my cramped and aching limbs. My assumption had been correct and as I turned the truck and headed back to Wedza, the first rays of the morning sun pierced the dawn to bathe the bleak countryside in its warm glow.

The results of the operation were inconclusive. Our 'terrorists' had been welcomed into the small village, but this didn't necessarily mean that the villagers were sympathisers as they could hardly turn away a group of heavily armed men. From information gleaned, there didn't appear to be any real terrorists in that immediate area.

The next day I was sent to pick up the previously deployed troops at the nearby misson. I drove up the same meandering sandy track as when I had deployed them except that it was now daylight and I noticed at one point piles of sand bags littering a bend. I was told later that this was where an ambush had taken place the previous year. The truck had been hit by an RPG 7 rocket and the driver killed.

The troopies had rounded up a dozen or so villagers for questioning and I noticed that, in contrast to Romeo Troop, they were far harsher in their treatment of the locals, manhandling them with a roughness I thought unnecessary. However, after questioning, enough information was amassed to enable Whiskey Troop to come into contact with a terrorist group a week after I had left. Romeo Troop in comparison had had a totally barren tour of duty.

Even in the midst of war however, there are examples of compassion. Just a few days before I was due to leave, a lone African man walked hesitantly into the camp to seek help. It turned out that his daughter had fallen awkwardly and had hurt her arm.

Taking a medic and escort we drove to his nearby village. Ever cautious of trouble however we left the vehicles at a safe distance and spread out in a wide arc to walk into the cluster of huts. There we found a piccanin aged about five years old. She regarded us with large wide eyes partly from fear of being surrounded by soldiers, and partly from pain. The medic confirmed that the arm was broken and tenderly made up a temporary splint. I was surprised to see the stick leader who, the previous day had been roughly herding the villagers onto the truck, gently calm the child and help carry her back to the truck. We then took her and her father the thirty or so kilometres to the small hospital at Wedza where we left them with smiles of gratitude.

The next day a strange incident took place. We received a radio call from the nearby INTAF fort to the effect that a group of terrorists were making their way towards the fort. The INTAF officer was almost hysterical as he pleaded for help. We rapidly despatched some troops, eager for some easy action, only to find that the 'terrorists' were his own District Assistants returning from their day out in the surrounding area. The loneliness of the job, or possibly the bottle, must have finally got to this officer. A job I was glad to have narrowly avoided when I was first called up.

Every time that we left the camp and drove up the dusty main street of the local village we had to drive round a thin, scrawny dog, stretched out fast asleep, oblivious to the goings on around him.

We made the same deviation around the prone form until one day

I stopped to see if he was alive. As I drew up alongside one bleary eye opened to see who had disturbed his dreams. Other than that there wasn't a flicker of movement. The eye closed and we left him to his slumbers.

Towards the end of my stint we ran out of fresh meat and our cook served up a very dark coloured stew, which was as tough as old boots and totally inedible. The meat had been purchased locally and some wit joked that it was probably the dog. Mysteriously, the following day the dog was missing from its usual sleeping place and we became perturbed when the road was still empty the day after that; you can imagine our relief however when, a few days later, the dormant canine reappeared.

Another tale didn't have such a happy ending however. On one night deployment I was slowly driving along an overgrown track when a serval cat darted out of the undergrowth. Despite the weight of the Puma I felt a definite jolt as the wheels rolled over it. I couldn't stop in time but, as we came to a halt, I heard a triumphant cry as one of the African troopies carried the limp carcase onto the truck. The next day he could be seen wearing, what looked like a Davy Crockett hat, with the poor cat's spotted tail hanging down his back. We rarely saw wild life so it was a great shame that this beautiful serval cat had decided, at that moment, to cross the road.

Throughout the whole stint I had driven over dry, dusty roads continually covered in clouds of dust thrown up by the escorting Hyena. Trying to avoid the choking atmosphere I covered my head with a balaclava and tied a clean handkerchief over my mouth and nose. Even so, my throat was so irritated by the dust particles that it became very sore and eventually I lost my voice. There was no hint of a cold or relevant sickness and as soon as I got back to tarred roads and clean air the soreness disappeared and my voice recovered.

Despite my apprehension, and the problems of being in such a remote camp, I had in fact enjoyed myself at 151 Charlie. With Romeo Troop and Whiskey Troop I had seen both sides of the coin. I had enjoyed both their company but Romeo Troop, led by a commander who was too nice to be in a war, working strictly by the book, had no success. Whiskey Troop however, rougher and harsher, although showing compassion when needed - as was seen with the injured child - had, as I heard later, a successful contact with five terrorists killed and a quantity of arms and equipment recovered.

CHAPTER 21

Tjotjolo

Although Support Unit was based at Tomlinson Depot in Salisbury, its duties extended throughout Rhodesia unless the area was controlled by the Army. Unlike any other Salisbury police reservists therefore, as Support Unit drivers, we could be posted to some most unlikely spots anywhere in the country. My next assignment was to Tjotjolo or Tjolotjo in the depths of Matabeleland, in the west, where ZIPRA terrorists, who were mainly Ndebeles, were the opposition. So far, in Mashonaland, we had been fighting ZANLA representing the Shonas. Occasionally the two factions would confront each other where their 'territories' overlapped.

Two weeks before Easter I consequently found myself in the company of John Whiteman, collecting tickets for the night train to Bulawayo. The rest of the day was free and so I went home to finish packing.

That evening we had a bleak farewell supper and then disaster struck. Two year old Michael was running around when he tripped over my outstretched feet and fell flat on his face. With wooden parquet flooring there was no protection, and he pushed his teeth through his lower lip. With blood pouring from the wound and mixing with his tears Vi rushed him to hospital. It was always hard to leave the family for a call up, but this time it was ten times worse, with a family crisis at the eleventh hour.

Fortunately, Vi made it back in time to accompany me to the station with a patched up son proudly displaying his injury. It was with a heavy heart, however, that I waved goodbye and watched the family group on the platform slowly diminish until the curve of the track hid them from sight.

John was good company and, after a couple of drinks in the buffet car, we retired to our compartment which had been rearranged by the steward as sleeping accommodation. The train travelled throughout the night, taking some twelve hours to cover the two hundred and sixty odd miles from Salisbury to Bulawayo. During the latter years of the war, progress was even slower, with the line being constantly checked for landmines, and the train would push two or three empty wagons ahead of it as a precaution against any explosions.

On arrival at Bulawayo we expected to find some form of transport awaiting us but, on checking, we could find no vehicle and there was no message at the station office. Undaunted, we phoned the main police station who, even though they hadn't a clue who we were, obligingly sent a police car to pick us up and take us to the police camp where we hoped to be able to radio either base camp. We were not perturbed by the disorganisation, it was after all, a typical SNAFU, similar to that which I have previously described.

As we drove through the busy streets of Saturday shoppers we suddenly espied a Support Unit Hyena in the traffic. We gave chase and soon pulled the vehicle over. The driver was relieved to see us and had only just arrived back in town from Tjotjolo where he had been told that we were expected the next morning. We assumed that the driver from the other camp was under the same impression and, as John was in no hurry to start his duties, I took over the vehicle. Stopping only to pick up some supplies from the local police depot, I was soon on my way. It was a long, straight, boring run about half way to Victoria Falls with no towns to break the monotony but the area was heavily wooded so it was not an unattractive drive.

Tjotjolo was situated a few kilometres north of Lupane, a small administration centre, where the land rises slightly forming a ridge or saddle between the Shangani river to the north and the Gwai river to the south. The camp was above a Tilcor agricultural development estate on land sloping down towards the Shangani. The managers and assistants houses were slightly below the camp and, on my first day, the Inspector in charge of the camp, known to everyone for obvious reasons as 'Ginger', took me down to the guest house, which was vacant, but boasted a swimming pool overlooking the surrounding countryside. As we lay in the sun, dozing off after a dip, it was absolutely idyllic looking out over the shimmering scene below.

There were two troops stationed at this camp although at that moment, with the exception of an escort troop, they were all deployed. Zulu Charlie troop were to be picked up the next day and would leave the camp for Salisbury the day after that.

After our swim we went down to the offices and workshop to meet the staff and then on down to some fields where the estate manager was overseeing a crop spraying operation.

Oblivious to what was going on, Ginger drove straight through the gateway onto the track edging the field, only to find the crop spraying aircraft already gaining momentum on its take off towards us. Ginger ditched the Land Rover and I caught a glimpse of the underside of the wing and rivets as the plane roared over us. The pilot was a New Zealander who travelled world wide to ply his trade and that evening he joined us, for an enjoyable few hours, at the manager's house where drinks and snacks were laid on.

The manager had, until recently, been farming his own spread nearby, but a terrorist raid had seen his house destroyed and his workforce driven off the land, although fortunately both he and his wife had survived unscathed.

I noticed that, besides the normal perimeter security fences, inside each room he had made tall, wheeled containers, filled with granite chippings, which were pushed across each window to stop sniper fire. He was obviously well experienced at anti-terrorist measures.

Before arriving, I expected to find a rather primitive camp but we were lucky to be on a large estate because, although we lived under canvas, the manager had organised fresh water to be piped up to the camp and had even built an ablution block with shower and flushing toilet.

The following morning I took a Puma to pick up Zulu Charlie Troop. We had no sooner reached the low level bridge over the Shangani than we realised it would be impossible to cross. The river had recently been coming down in flood and all that could be seen of the bridge was a furrow in the swollen muddy water as it swept past towards the Zambezi. On the far bank we could see two stationary buses, the occupants of which were gazing despondently at the flood. We retraced our steps up river to where a weir had been built as part of the irrigation scheme for the estate. The only way of crossing the river in its present state was by a small rowing boat on the slightly calmer water above the weir. Returning to the camp, we called up Zulu Charlie troop and radioed through the information regarding the river. The news was not accepted with very good grace as the troop would now have a few hours trek to the boat. On the other side of the ridge the Gwai river was also in flood so it looked as though this would be a quiet stay with no troops able to deploy. My prediction was to be proved wrong however.

By evening the whole of the Zulu Charlie troop had slowly returned to camp. They had a day to kill before moving out to return for R & R in Salisbury and this proved to be a day I would rather forget.

I had already heard of their Troop Commander by reputation. He was a big, unpleasant, almost psychopathic man and there were many rumours as to his methods of interrogation and even of his handling of his own troops. He was brash and arrogant and, I discovered shortly after meeting him, we had a mutual acquaintance who was a very good friend of mine. Such was his nature however that he immediately started to run down, and virtually character assassinate, the friend in his absence. It was quite obvious from the start that you could not reason with this man and, in fact, I am sure that, like any bully, he did it deliberately to provoke a reaction. I decided to ignore his outspoken comments as I had already seen evidence of his unreasonable behaviour.

I had noticed a small transistor radio on the dining table with a large hole in the centre. It turned out that a few days before I had arrived he, with various others, had been sitting in the mess tent listening to the radio when a political comment regarding the Rhodesian situation, contrary to his own views, was expressed on the news. In a fit of temper he picked up his sawn off shot gun, (he didn't carry a regulation weapon like the rest of us) and blasted the transistor radio. One of the troopies sitting immediately opposite, who was under no illusions as to the man's character, fortunately realised what was about to happen and threw himself to the floor. At such close range the blast blew a neat hole about 35 millimetres in diameter through the radio, ripped the recently vacated opposite chair to shreds and put out of action a deep freeze behind the chair. To call it foolhardy would be an understatement. The man had a definite mental problem. As there was no-one of higher rank the incident passed and I have no knowledge as to whether it was ever reported.

Anyway, back to the day in question. Beers and brandy appeared shortly after breakfast so the rest of us decided to keep a low profile and stayed out of the way as far as possible. At one stage empty beer cans were tossed in the air while the sawn off shot gun was fired indiscriminately in an effort to prove what a good shot he was. Occasionally he would seek us out, wherever we had sought refuge, taunt us with offers of drink and, on our refusal, demand to know why we would not drink with him. The party went on throughout the day and well into the small hours of the morning so it was with bleary eyes that we watched with relief as they straggled out of the camp, heading back to Salisbury, the next day.

That evening we were back to work and I followed an escort vehicle south past Lupane until we turned off the main road and headed north east towards the small township of Kenmaur. We seemed to drive for hours over the rough dirt roads with the Hyena, ahead, occasionally stopping to call up and trace the troop we were picking up. At one stage we stopped at a large road maintenance camp; the graders and bulldozers lit up garishly in a blaze of security lights.

We managed to find some personnel to get fresh directions and still we moved on until I felt as though I was in a dream. The black night sky seemed to merge with the road ahead and it felt as though we were suspended in space. The only real world was within my cab. Suddenly I snapped back to reality. The blackness was very real, in fact it was flood water from the Lupane river. The road was slightly higher than the surrounding land and the black menacing water was just beginning to swirl around my wheels.

The Hyena stopped and, conversing over the radio, we decided to proceed one at a time and, if possible, always keep one vehicle on solid ground, in case the other needed rescuing. The Hyena set off, churning through the flood water like a paddle steamer. At one point it rose majestically out of the flood as it negotiated a small bridge that stood stark and grotesque in the middle of the black liquid. As the Hyena almost disappeared from my headlight beams the message came through that it had reached dry land. Now it was my turn to brave the swirling waters and it felt strange having no road or verges to be able to orientate myself. I concentrated my gaze on the bridge railings ahead and prayed that the road was straight. It was an eerie experience at night to have no landmarks to navigate by.

Soon after the flooded area we found the missing troopies. We loaded up quickly as I was worried that the flood waters may have risen too high for our return but my fears were unfounded and a few hours later we were safely back in the camp.

The new troop to replace Zulu Charlie arrived the next day with a bang. An errant bee had flown into the open cockpit of the troop leader's Land Rover and, as he desperately groped between his legs to evict the invader, he lost control and rammed a tree. The result was a bent bumper and mudguard but no injuries; not even a bee sting.

We had a resident mechanic to look after the maintenance of our vehicles but, unlike Van at 151 Alpha who itched to see some action, this one spent most of his time in Bulawayo on the pretext of picking up spare parts. I think I saw him once during my two week stint so consequently I spent my spare time rectifying a fuel starved Land Rover and misfiring Bedford. The latter gave me a heart stopping return from Lupane late one afternoon when it began running so badly that I was reduced to a walking pace. I had inadvertently left my tools back at the camp and, as the sun dropped lower over the horizon and the evening shadows lengthened, it became a nerve wracking drive. We eventually made it back to the camp in the twilight to the relief of the camp commander who was as worried as I had been.

One day we received a call from the police at Lupane to the effect that there appeared to be some local unrest because some trees had been cut down to form a roadblock. We immediately deployed to the area which was towards St. Paul's mission where we did indeed find the road blocked, but not by a few trees. The road literally disappeared beneath hundreds of horizontal trunks and branches. It must have taken days to cause such destruction to the forest and the job of clearance was far bigger than we had first anticipated.

At first the locals pleaded ignorance to the arboreal carnage a few yards from their homes but eventually admitted that a group of terrorists had cajoled the locals into taking this action which, they thought, would have the effect of slowing down the deployment of troops into the area. However, the villagers had only succeeded in giving themselves a lot of hard work to do as our troops immediately seconded them all as labourers to start clearing up the mess.

Three days later I was called back to St. Paul's mission to pick up our troops. No ters had been found but now the road was passable. Some of the larger trees had been left and a track cut through the bush around them. This was rather unnerving as we were not sure whether this was possibly a new road block with the continued risk of landmines or ambush. Consequently the going was slow as we had to de-bus troops to check the track ahead and sweep through the forest on either side.

At one point the road followed close by the course of the Shangani river and, arriving at the mission, we were within a few miles of the site of a conflict enacted some eighty years previously. A patrol, led by Major Alan Wilson, in search of Chief Lobengula during the Matabele War of 1892 had been surrounded by Ndebele warriors and massacred. History records that, as their comrades fell and the ammunition had run low, the few remaining officers had sat back to back, singing hymns, expending their last shots until they had all breathed their last. It seemed ironic that men had once again taken up arms and were at conflict in this beautiful land.

After what seemed an age, we arrived at the abandoned mission of St. Pauls. Because of the terrorist situation the priests had been forced to leave some months before and the destruction was appalling. Not only was the chapel and school ransacked but the small hospital and operating theatre had been wrecked. A large amount of equipment had been left behind and what looked like an X-ray machine lay smashed as had all the other amenities. It was pointless vandalism because the Catholic mission was there solely to help the local African population.

As our troops climbed aboard the truck they appeared more restrained than usual as if subdued by seeing such wanton destruction.

Letting the clutch out to leave the pitiful scene, I was restrained by a yell from behind. I stopped, and one of the troop leaders ran back to where a large crucifix lay face down in the dirt. With reverence he picked it up and propped it against a nearby wall. It was touching to see this rough, war-hardened young man carry out this act of devotion.

There is always a chance, when being in such close proximity with virtual strangers, that there will be a clash of personalities. At most of the camps in which I had resided, we had all got on reasonably well. In this camp there had been the unfortunate business with the psychopathic leader of Zulu Charlie Troop and now Ginger, the camp commander, was becoming a bit of a bore. Having been removed from active duty, because of health reasons, he vented his frustration on the younger conscripts and, while denigrating them, never missed an opportunity of boasting about his prowess in past contacts with the enemy. Most of his tales were obviously exaggerated and rather too far fetched. He was forever organising training sessions to prove his expertise with grenades and mortars. One day he returned from giving a demonstration to some local farmers and we were intrigued to see him hobble from his Land Rover with one foot heavily bandaged like an ex-army Colonel suffering from gout. It transpired that, while demonstrating a mortar, he had got over confident, discarded the base plate and fired the apparatus while resting the tube against his foot. Unfortunately for him, the reaction of firing the mortar had forced the tube onto his foot and, in so doing, had broken a couple of toes. We heard no more boasting as he sulked in reaction to our hilarity.

A couple of days before the end of my stint we took two Pumas and a complete troop to deploy north past Gwai village at Lubimbi Hot Springs. By coincidence, some five years before, I had met the owner and manager of the small hotel which had been built near the springs, when his car had broken down whilst on a visit to Salisbury. He had insisted that if I was ever in the area, to drop in, as the hot springs were marvellous.

I hadn't expected to drop in under the present circumstances but when we arrived it quickly became obvious that the hotel complex had been abandoned for some time. A few ramshackle buildings remained, their skeletal roof timbers staring skywards, the corrugated iron sheeting probably now adorning a neighbouring kraal. As if to emphasise the desolation, it started to rain with steam from the natural hot springs fighting against the elements.

Leading the way I left the complex behind us and followed a track which was fast becoming a stream. We hadn't gone very far however, when a message over the radio informed me that the Puma following had become stuck in the mud. I stopped on firm ground and walked back, my heart sinking as soon as I saw it. It was already bogged down deeply and, as we watched, the weight of the armour plating made it sink even further. With what equipment we had with us, we quickly chopped down the straightest trees that we could find and, after trimming off the branches, placed them under the chassis in a desperate attempt to spread the weight and arrest the decline. We appeared to have driven over a patch of quicksand because as we walked near the vehicle, the ground wobbled like a jelly from water saturation.

After a few futile attempts to dig the Puma out, it was decided that I should take an escort back to the base camp and return with the four wheel drive Bedford and whatever equipment I could lay my hands on to extricate the vehicle. The first problem was to retrace my steps back past the stranded Puma, so it was with extreme caution that we checked the ground as I made a detour through the virgin bush.

It was dark by the time I arrived back at camp so it wasn't until the next day that I was able to return. After hours of cutting wood to lay as a mat and digging trenches, we were at a stage to be able to try pulling her out. Fortunately, at the first attempt, everyone was standing well back because, with a chain linking the two vehicles, I took the strain with the Bedford in reverse, low range and four wheel drive. Suddenly one of the links snapped and the chain snaked back like elastic. If anyone had been standing near, the force would have broken a leg or worse. More digging and more chopping ensued and then we tried again. This time, with loud sucking noises, the mud relinquished its hold.

During that day I had noticed that my rifle butt had worked loose and, on closer inspection back at camp, I discovered that it had broken, rendering the firearm useless. It was with some trepidation therefore that I set out unarmed the next day on my return trip to Bulawayo, particularly when the Hyena I was driving developed a misfire and I was forced to stop in a lonely area to tighten the distributor that had shaken loose. I was greatly relieved to reach the outskirts of the city and within an hour or so I was sitting having a meal with friends before boarding the train for the last leg of my trip.

I had heard reports of heavy rain and flooding near Salisbury and, as the train neared Lake McIlwaine, it slowed to a walking pace and I was amazed to see the washaway which, a few days previously, had derailed a goods train into the quagmire below.

An emergency track had literally been laid over some of the wagons which had sunk deep in the mud and, as we negotiated the hazard, it was intriguing to see the roofs and wagon sides of the derailed train below us.

CHAPTER 22

A South African Intermission

Despite the influence of the war on our lives, or possibly because of it, there was a strange normality to civilian life. The commercial and industrial life carried on as well as it could under the circumstances of sanctions and staff call ups. Clubs and associations still organised meetings. In the cities, the cinemas, restaurants and night clubs thrived; social life in general buzzed with activity.

For many years I had been involved with motor sport and, some years earlier, I had acquired a very rare ex-works Austin Healey 100S.

The nearest Austin Healey Car Club was in Johannesburg some 1200 kilometres away in South Africa and, at Easter in 1978, the Club decided to organise a social weekend at Louis Trichard, a small town within 160 kilometres of the Rhodesian border. This was an opportunity, not only to meet other club members, but would be an exciting weekend for my children, who now rarely left the confines of the city. Currency restrictions being what they were, we decided to plan the trip to give us the maximum possible time in South Africa with the least possible expense.

We left Salisbury early on Good Friday, accompanied by another club member, Dave Harrup. We towed the Healey on a trailer for convenience and the first 200 kilometres passed without incident. At the small mining town of Umvuma we caught up with the first armed convoy which took us into Fort Victoria.

The convoys travelled at about 100 kph and although we were pulling the trailer, we managed to keep up and things were going well - or so we thought. As we pulled into a petrol station to refuel I heard a strange scraping noise from the trailer and further investigation revealed a collapsed wheel bearing.

With only fifteen minutes to go before the departure of the next convoy some quick thinking was indicated. We would have to drive the Healey the rest of the way so it was off loaded and, finding a yard in which to leave the trailer, managed to reach the convoy collection point with both cars and just two minutes to spare.

A few days before leaving on this trip I had the presence of mind to surreptitiously 'borrow' an Uzi sub machine gun from the Support Unit armoury but, as we were the last to arrive, we were placed at the back of the convoy where we were well protected by the Browning machine gun mounted on the Mazda pickup truck immediately behind us.

Having spent two weeks on this convoy, I knew the road like the back of my hand, but gazing over the louvred aluminium bonnet of a sports car at the shimmering road ahead was in sharp contrast to looking down the barrel of a Browning machine gun, as I had during my stint on the convoy a year before . This was the most dangerous part of the trip, with a number of incidents having occurred previously on this 250 kilometre stretch of road.

It was midday and the sun blazed down on to the open top sports car and, as we dropped down into the lowveld, the temperature must have been at least 35oC in the shade. As for Dave and me, we were being burnt to a crisp behind the low perspex windscreen. While driving on this long, hot stretch my thoughts went back to 1954 when this particular car was first built to compete in the Mille Miglia and wondered if, in the wildest stretches of their imagination, anyone then could have visualised one of their team cars, nearly twenty five years later, being driven through a war zone in Africa in an armed convoy with spotter aircraft flitting overhead and the driver armed with a sub-machine gun.

Late that afternoon we arrived at Beit Bridge, the border town where we were to stay the night, thus saving some of our precious foreign currency.

A crowd of motor bikers had arrived from South Africa and as some of the 'Hells Angel' looking riders swaggered into the reception toting revolvers and pistols, obviously showing off their bravery at having entered the 'war zone', I was booking my sub-machine gun into the strong room. The wind was taken out of their sails at seeing an ordinary family man with a bigger gun than theirs, and they retired quietly to the corner of the bar.

The next morning, and to save currency once again, we left the family saloon at the hotel. Dave had to hitch hike from now on and the family squeezed into the Healey. After crossing the border we stopped at Messina to do some shopping. Sanctions did not affect our daily lives at all, but there were shortages of luxury goods, so consequently some of our precious foreign currency was spent on such things as smoked oysters, wine and Easter eggs for the children. Then it was on to our hotel high in the mountains overlooking Louis Trichard and the plain below that shimmered to the horizon.

The weekend was spent in good company with the war and all the problems it brought, left in another world. Alas it was over all too soon and on the Sunday afternoon we left our new made friends to retrace our steps and re-cross the border to spend another night at the hotel before rejoining the convoy for the return trip at 7.00a.m. on Monday morning.

At Fort Victoria I decided to risk collecting the trailer and taking it home unloaded. I followed behind Vi for the remainder of the trip and, despite a wobbling wheel, we made it safely home.

The next weekend, as I jacked up the trailer to change the bearing, the wheel gracefully tipped over and fell off!

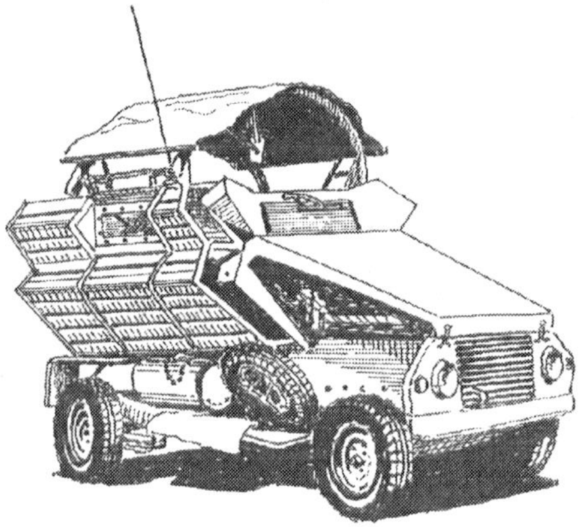

CHAPTER 23

Mrewa

Mrewa was an administrative centre about 50 kilometres from Mtoko and approximately 70 kilometres north of Salisbury. It was no more than a village, comprising the District Commissioners office and council workshops, police station, post office and a dozen or so houses for the relevant employees. At one end of the village there was a sports club with swimming pool and tennis court. In more peaceful times I had spent a day at the club when I had bought a car from a local resident. At the opposite end of the village were the shops which mainly catered for the African trade from the surrounding area.

The Support Unit camp was based in a large compound within the precincts of the police camp and was surrounded by the obligatory high security fence.

The officer in charge at the camp was one I had not met before. He was a serious, aloof person who used his rank to distance himself from the troops and in particular, as it soon became apparent, from the transport drivers who were mere 'reservists'.

There were two drivers stationed at Mrewa at any one time. Each being on a two week tour, but one changed every week so that there was an overlap of one driver which gave continuity. This was of particular help with knowledge of the local area.

Phil was the driver already halfway through his stint when I arrived.

I had never worked with him before and, right from the word go, we got on very well together. Phil was a natural comedian and for his remaining week I don't think I had ever laughed so much since my first call up.

Within hours of my arrival a report came in of a terrorist sighting in the local beer hall. We quickly deployed a section of India troop but there was no sign of the suspect. The troop decided to make a sweep through the kraals to the east where another report came of suspect movement. Normally, Phil and I would have driven back to camp, leaving the troops to get on with their job. This time, however, the troop leader asked if we would like to tag along. I looked at Phil, he looked at me.

"Why not? It's better than sitting around in the camp."

We left a guard with the trucks and joined in the line about 100 metres across and started the sweep. I had naively thought that we were in for a pleasant stroll through the country with the possibility of some excitement. It wasn't to be however, as India troop started a fast sweep and even walking in a straight line isn't as easy as it sounds. The season at that time of the year was spring and the bush appeared green and smooth, but as we walked we came across barbed wire fences, ditches, thick bushes and, at one time, glutinous mud as we walked across a vlei running with water. At one stage the mud sucked off one of Phil's boots and he overbalanced while trying to retrieve it.

We were splattered with mud, our clothes soaked and the pace was so fast I hadn't time to look for suspicious movement anywhere. Wide eyed piccanins ran screaming to their mothers as we stumbled past clumps of mud huts until, with great relief, we eventually gained the hard dusty surface of a road. We had travelled in a wide arc and now had about three and a half kilometres to hobble back to the trucks. The regular troops were hardly breathing above normal, while Phil and I puffed and wheezed behind them, helping each other along, feet sore with blisters that were already forming in our wet and muddy boots.

Back at camp we eased our aching feet in bowls of cold water and ruefully reflected on our fitness compared to the regular troops who could have kept up a march throughout the whole day and, even now, to add insult to injury, were enjoying a game of volleyball.

South of Mrewa lay a large mission called St. Pauls. I suppose that there are only so many saint's names to go round, because in virtually every area I went into there was a St. Pauls Mission.

A few months earlier a gang of terrorists had arrived at the mission, dragged the priests into the garden where they were tied up and shot. One priest survived the massacre and, despite the terrible slaughter, the mission had carried on, with the churchmen, administering to the local population, totally unmoved.

One night we were sent to deploy nearby. Navigation was always difficult at night, unless one knew the area, and we mistook a Y junction for another further on and took the wrong road. Phil was ahead in the Puma, while I followed on in a Bedford RM when suddenly his truck lurched to a stop. He had narrowly avoided driving into a deep crevice, where the road had been washed away, and we could go no further. Consulting the map by torch-light we realised our mistake and started to turn the vehicles. On the narrow track this was easier said than done and we ended up having to reverse in the pitch black back to the Y junction.

We had barely covered half a kilometre when the Puma's engine cut out. For the next half an hour or so we tried, with what few tools we possessed, to restart the engine but to no avail. By now, from the noise we were making, I am sure that any terrorist in the vicinity would have been alerted to our presence. We were only a few kilometres from the drop off point but the troops refused to walk the extra distance so, after some argument, it ended up with me shuttling to and fro with the troops to a nearby river crossing. Although it was extremely dangerous to continually retrace my steps like that, there couldn't have been a ter within many kilometres as we eventually completed the deployment without incident.

Dawn was breaking by the time we arrived back at the camp having left a guard with the disabled Puma. We weren't to sleep for long though as, within a couple of hours of our return, the camp commander stormed into our tent demanding to know why we had left a vehicle out in the bush all night. He was a 'book' policeman and this was evidently against one of the rules.

Every now and then you would run into one of these higher ranking officers who forgot that they were not dealing with conscripts straight from school. Generally the transport drivers seconded to Support Unit were men in their thirties and forties, quite often holding very responsible jobs in civvy street and we were quite capable of making our own decisions. I suppose in some ways it was difficult for them to accept that we were 'different', we did have to abide by the rules and regulations, but they had not got the hold over us that they had over the regular troops and some of them just did not know how to handle it.

We let him bluster on for a bit and then he left. After breakfast I went round to the workshops to see the mechanic who maintained the vehicles on camp. He, however, refused point blank to come out to the stranded Puma and it soon became obvious that he was absolutely petrified of leaving the comparative safety of Mrewa village. Once again the complete opposite of dear old Van at 151 Alpha.

It eventually ended up with Phil and I taking some chains with us and towing the Puma back. It was a long, tiring run but, despite the danger of ambush, you couldn't suppress Phil's sense of humour as he insisted, when calling me on the radio, in announcing, "Mobile One, this is Immobile Two."

A few days later, the troops that we had deployed called in. Despite the disastrous deployment, they had had a contact and were awaiting a pick-up. Arriving at the rendezvous point we saw a donkey cart with some locals talking to the troops. Reclining in the back of the cart were three dead ters. One was a particularly gruesome sight, having taken the full force of a machine gun. A number of AK assault rifles, grenades, mines and ammunition had been recovered. What had started out as a disaster had ended up a success and we were forgiven.

The countryside around Mrewa was typically Rhodesian. Undulating grass and woodland interspersed with rocky kopjes and the occasional granite 'gomo' A few kilometres from Mrewa there rose the grandfather of all 'gomos', its grey sides rising vertically like the ramparts of a medieval castle. I learnt later that our radio link was established on top of this small mountain. The radio operators had to be flown in by helicopter to avoid the difficult climb. The surrounding land was very sandy and the narrow tracks that we drove along meandered their way around the various kopjes and obstacles.

I had never been in an area where the protected village system was so complete. We would drive past deserted huts and kraals with only the occasional local tilling the fields, then suddenly come across a vast security fenced area containing hundreds of huts set out in neat rows. Often the road would dissect the village and guards would open and close the gates as we passed through. Anti-propaganda labelled these villages as concentration camps, but all of those that I saw looked neat and tidy, fresh water was supplied and the people appeared to be happy, with piccanins laughing and playing. The occupants were free to move in and out of the compound during the day, to attend to their crops and animals, provided that they were back inside in time for the curfew.

The curfew was imposed on those parts of the country where the terrorist activity was at its fiercest. If any unexplained movement was seen between dusk and dawn, the security forces could open fire without warning. The adverse side of the curfew, however, was the fact that security force movement had to be more closely monitored than usual to avoid accidental contact with our own side. The terrorists had the advantage of being warned of our presence, as we were the only ones allowed free movement. Because of this, we sometimes carried out daytime deployments.

One night there was a near disaster after a call was received from a farmer who had seen movement outside his compound. We despatched a couple of sticks to investigate, only to find that this movement was being caused by a police unit which specialised in tracking cattle rustlers. No-one had thought to inform the farmer or other security force units in the area that they were going in and fortunately no shots were fired.

Cattle rustling had grown to almost epidemic proportions and the cost to the farmers and the economy as a whole was astronomical. The cattle were stolen either to feed the terrorists or to swell the herds of the local population.

The anti-rustling unit, for some reason we couldn't understand, had precedence over Support Unit and, at times, we would put troops into the bush only to have to pull them out again within a few hours. The clash became so bad that Mrewa camp eventually closed down.

In general, despite the confines of a base camp, we all got on fairly well together although the ages ranged from raw seventeen year old conscripts to forty year old drivers. Some were regular troops and others, like the drivers and some radio operators, were reservists, but we all mixed in well. There is a lot of waiting around in any war and this one was no different, we spent many amicable times sitting around chatting and the conversation was probably more interesting and lively because of the differences in age and experience. Sometimes though, we would come up against a regular troopie who didn't fit in because he was seemingly overawed with his own importance and try to pull rank. There was just such a troop leader on this camp, younger than the average for his rank and rather prone to being overweight and extremely arrogant. He would cut us out of any gathering or conversation and try to ridicule us 'amateur' reservists.

On one occasion I had the misfortune to have him on the back of my truck. As I sat in the cab of the Bedford RM waiting for the off, the passenger door was flung open and the troop leader, without asking, dumped all his kit onto the passenger seat and floor. Before I could protest the door was slammed shut followed by the command to move out.

This really annoyed me because, despite the fact that I didn't like the man anyway, the cab of the truck was supposed to be kept clear. If we hit a landmine these innocuous looking objects could become lethal projectiles and. in the case of an ambush, could block my escape from the cab.

Although annoyed, I decided not to protest and followed Phil out of the camp and through Mrewa village. We had barely covered a few kilometres when there was a bang on the cab roof and a bossy shout of."Driver, you're too close to the truck in front!"

That really hit the spot and my temper flared. Radioing Phil that I was stopping, I pulled up sharply in a swirl of dust. Without saying a word I climbed down from the cab, walked round to the passenger side, removed the kit and, with one swing, hurled it up onto the back where the troop leader sat open mouthed.

"Careful, you'll damage something." he spluttered.

"Shut up!" I roared. "If you want to work strictly to the rules then so will I. From now on no kit is to be put into my cab!"

He attempted to protest but I cut him short.

"I'm in charge of this truck and I do not expect interference with my driving from behind. Understand?"

With a feeble nod he agreed and from that moment I had no more trouble from him. By coincidence he was at 151 Alpha a few weeks later and he greeted me like an old friend, even popping into our tent for a chat in the evenings.

During the hours we spent sitting around and waiting for action Phil was really good company and we chatted and laughed many hours away. There were also volley ball games and, at this camp, the sparse village to wander around. Each day I would wander down to the Post Office and put a call through to home where Vi would keep me up to date on any news.

On one of these typical days, whilst rummaging through our rations, we found a typed recipe list and so decided to while away a few hours by doing some cooking. We settled on oatmeal pancakes, which sounded delicious and, checking that we had the ingredients, set to work. Unfortunately there were one or two plastic packs which were not labelled. One could easily distinguish salt from sugar but we ended up with two bags of brownish grain, neither of which we could identify as oatmeal. After some discussion, we made a decision and a short time later we were sampling the results of our handiwork. The taste was not quite right, but they were edible and we soon scoffed the lot.

For the next few days we both suffered badly from constipation. It later dawned on us that we had mistakenly used a fine grain semolina instead of oatmeal when we made our pancakes.

Phil's tour of duty had drawn to a close and on Saturday Koos Swanapeol arrived. I knew him from a previous call up and, although he was pleasant company, the instant puns and hilarity had left with Phil.

Almost immediately we received a call that an INTAF truck had been ambushed. The alarm had been raised when the truck had arrived in the village having sustained a few bullet holes. Nobody was hurt but one of the labourers, who had been on the back of the truck, was missing. No-one knew if he had been hit or whether he had fallen off in the excitement.

We drove to the ambush point but there was no sign of the man or, for that matter, any blood. A scattering of spent bullet cases betrayed the position from where the terrorists had fired. Spoor, unfortunately, was non-existent and so we started a search of the surrounding countryside. The huts and kraals were, as usual, totally deserted.

Driving slowly back towards Mrewa we checked each building for our missing soul but to no avail. He could have been abducted, which was happening a lot at that time, or led away to be murdered elsewhere.

Back at the camp we made our dismal report, only to find out that the absentee had run into the INTAF offices within a short while of us leaving. It turned out that he had fallen off the back of the truck with shock, picked himself up and run the four or five kilometres at Olympic speed.

Because of the problems of deploying in a curfew area we weren't doing much night work and so fortunately we were getting a good nights sleep most nights. I must have been asleep for a few hours one night when I gradually became conscious of some distant shouting. I couldn't hear what was being said but it appeared to be an argument of some kind.

Grabbing our rifles, Koos and I stealthily made our way outside to the camp perimeter where a small enquiring group had already gathered. The shouting was coming from the living quarters of the main police camp and, by now, the gist of the argument was becoming clear.

"You bastard, I'll teach you to mess about with my wife when I'm away."

"Calm down, nothing's going on," came the lower tones of someone trying to defuse the situation.

"Fuck off you bastard. I'm going to kill you."

"Don't do anything stupid," a different voice interjected, so there were at least three people there.

The altercation died down to mumbling tones and then, just as we thought it was all over, the shouting became more urgent.

"Get your hands off me or I'll kill the lot of you," and with that outburst the unmistakable metallic clunk of a rifle being cocked could clearly be heard in the still night air. As one we all dropped to the ground. If there was going to be any wild firing we didn't want to get in the way of a stray bullet.

There were sounds of a scuffle and sharp exchanges.

"It's all right, I've got his rifle. Now piss off, don't come round here drunk and threatening us. Nothing is going on with your wife. Do you understand? Bugger off."

A car door slammed and lights appeared. At breakneck speed a car hurtled down the drive until, with a grinding crash, it struck one of the large, concrete gate posts. Shadowy forms could be seen running down the road, the driver was pulled out and the engine switched off. The remaining lights were doused and, in the evening silence the only sound was sobbing.

"My wife, my car..............." his drunken fury and frustration subsiding into self pity and remorse.

We never did find out the whole story and in fact it wasn't our place to know. It was just an example of how the nervous tension that we lived under could explode at any time.

I have mentioned previously the strains marriages were under at this time. It was said that a good marriage could only get stronger under these circumstances, but it was still worrying to realise the unreal situation that we lived in and often ones thoughts turned to the family at home.

A couple of days before the end of my stint we were called out to assist with a contact at the Shavanhohwe river. The Rhodesian African Rifles, assisted by the Air Force, were engaged in a battle with a number of ters. We were to take a truck with extra fuel for the helicopter gunships if required. In past years the river had been a favourite picnic spot for me and I knew the area well. The particular place that we were heading towards was the old low level bridge, overlooked by three towering granite gomos. The river lazily wound past the foot of these monoliths with sandy shores, interspersed with rock pools, leading further downstream to a picturesque waterfall. Memories flooded back of better days, including climbing each of these gomos to admire the spectacular views from the top.

The contact was some way down stream but we parked within sight of the gomos. A wave of melancholy swept over me, being in a place with too many memories, which now was a stage for death and destruction.

There wasn't much time for personal thoughts however, as the first helicopter dropped in for refuelling. From then on we were kept busy and it wasn't until much later that my thoughts returned to those happier days.

"I'm glad to leave those bloody hills behind," a troopie was saying." What a climb, they're bloody high you know," the last sentence addressed to me.

"I know," I replied. "You don't have to tell me, I've been to the top of all those hills in past years."

"What for?" he asked incredulously.

"For fun, and to see the view," I replied, knowing that he wouldn't understand the affection I held for this beautiful countryside. It was useless to explain when caught up in a war situation.

I was glad to leave Mrewa because, although there had been lighter moments with Phil, these had been counter balanced by the unpleasantness of the C.O. and boorishness of a certain troop leader and also by the feeling that we were not being allowed to do our job properly.

A few days after I had returned home, Koos was ambushed close to where the INTAF truck had been attacked. He was leading another vehicle on the way back to camp when he had to traverse a badly muddied section of road. When he was in the middle of the quagmire the ters opened up with small arms fire and Koos had the horror of getting bogged down in the middle of the killing zone. It was only the presence of mind of the following driver, who bravely stopped alongside for Koos to transfer to the other vehicle, that saved him. Miraculously no-one was injured.

I had been in the first batch of Transport drivers to be seconded to Support Unit and I had now been working in the front line for just over a year. Many drivers had been involved in incidents, driving over landmines or being ambushed but no-one, to my knowledge, had been killed or seriously injured. I had been extremely lucky, because incidents had happened either days before I arrived at a camp, or days after leaving so I had missed them all. How much longer could my luck hold out?

CHAPTER 24

The Abduction

The day hadn't started off at all well and I hoped that it wasn't an omen for the whole call up.

On arriving at Tomlinson Depot I had met my driving partner, Jack, who appeared to be a pleasant, middle aged man, but he had only just finished his basic training and this was, in fact, his first tour of duty. This annoyed me slightly as, with the war hotting up more and more as each day passed, Support Unit deserved more experienced drivers.

His presence probably reflected a growing problem, that there were more people leaving the country than ever before. Almost a thousand a month were departing for good and this became known as 'taking the gap' or 'the chicken run'.

Trying to hide my annoyance I greeted him as amicably as possible but his total lack of experience meant that the full onus of responsibility for each deployment and movement of vehicles was placed fairly and squarely on my shoulders. Perhaps I was becoming a little war weary but I didn't relish the thought of the next two weeks.

We picked up a newly refurbished Hyena and set off, but it wasn't until we stopped at the troops canteen in Marandellas, for some refreshment that I realised, with some alarm, that I had forgotten to collect our fresh rations. There was nothing for it but to turn back, as otherwise we would have very little food for the next two weeks. We always had large compo packs containing a variety of tinned food and powdered cereals and milk but without the fresh stores our meals would be a bit grim. I cursed myself for having forgotten an errand that I had done dozens of times before.

The Quartermaster's storemen were surprised to see us so late but we quickly loaded up and, as we attempted to leave, the starter motor on the Hyena gave a mournful clunk and stopped working. The engine would not turn over and more precious minutes were wasted as we eventually had to push start the Hyena, but from then on I could not switch off the engine for fear of not being able to restart. By now we were over two hours late and, as we passed the small settlement of Headlands, I started to hear excited jabbering over the radio. We were still too far from 151 Alpha to make out the incoherent messages but, as we got closer, it became obvious that something serious was afoot.

As I drove, with some trepidation, through the camp entrance, Fred Mason came rushing out.

"Where the hell have you been," he shouted, and in the same breath. "Never mind now. Get your kit unloaded, we've got to get moving. Hurry!'

I found, to my great relief, that there was a third driver there, called Roy, who had finished one week with one more to go. He gave us a brief run down on the situation.

A farmer, by the name of Christian, had been abducted by a small group of terrorists. The trackers employed in the follow up indicated that the terrorists and their hostage were now heading towards our area on their way to the border with Mocambique.

This was a ruse that the terrorists occasionally employed. Usually they would abduct African school children to be taken across the border, for training as terrorists, but occasionally a white farmer or government employee would be snatched. We knew from a previous briefing that the terrorist's ultimate prize was to kidnap a member of the security forces. That information certainly didn't help our nerves when driving in some of the more lonely and desolate parts of the war zone, but they never achieved their ambition, although one white government employee had been abducted a few years back and it wasn't until a year later that he turned up, over a thousand miles away, in Tanzania!

These abductions had the joint effect of tying up a vast number of the security forces in follow up operations and, as the abductions were normally successful, it was of great propaganda value. In other words, they were proving that they held power and could run circles around our security forces.

Galling though it was to realise this, it was quite true, as I do not recall any abductors being caught or their prisoners being rescued.

The next few days were spent continually keeping fresh trackers on the scent and setting up observation posts ahead of the likely route of the group. It was a problem trying to spot them, as they mainly moved at night and holed up during the day. It was tiring work for us as we had to move at a moments notice anytime, twenty four hours a day.

Our only vague chance was that Mr Christian was an elderly man and reputed to have heart trouble who could not move very quickly so the group would not be able to move as fast as normal. The ters would be desperate to keep him alive because, once over the border in Mozambique, he would be paraded before the terrorist camps as a great propaganda prize.

As each day passed, so Fred Mason's temper got shorter. Before this kidnapping there hadn't been much action for some weeks and, even now, the large wall map in the ops room was devoid of any terrorist sightings, which made things even more frustrating because it was obvious that in the area up on the wall, were the ominous hidden movements of the abductors.

On one of our trips, to pick up members of an Observation Post, we drove down a familiar dirt road in the Makoni TTL. I was in the leading Puma, with Jack behind and we drove past the village and school where, just a year ago, we had watched the contact in the valley below and where I had got so uptight at my first sight of a terrorist when a prisoner had been flown in. Suddenly my attention returned to the job in hand as I approached a large hole in the road and, from the remains of a wheel and metal parts on the verge, obviously a land mine crater. My senses were keen as I slowed and scanned the road ahead.

Another crater suddenly loomed up in front of me, and another, and still another. I was horrified to think of the number of times I had driven up and down this hitherto peaceful road which now reflected past carnage and an escalation in terrorist activity. After the sixth crater I decided that discretion was the better part of valour so I turned off the road to drive over the lightly tilled fields and rough verge. We only had about a kilometre to go to the pick up point and when we had stopped Jack immediately asked me why we had taken to the fields.

"Did you see those holes dotted around in the road?" I asked and he nodded.

"Well," I continued. "Those were landmine craters and I didn't want to risk hitting a forgotten mine."

He paled visibly as the reality of being in the front line of the war came home to him. We retraced our steps, closely following our own tracks but Jack was now lagging behind, driving at no more more than a walking pace. I called him up over the radio.

"What's the trouble?"

"I'm looking for marks in the road which might be a landmine."

"Don't worry about that," I replied. "Keep in my wheel tracks and, as I'm in front, the odds are far greater that I'll hit one before you."

I tried to sound casual but I was tensed up, squinting at the road ahead. I pulled the full harness seat belt tighter, at least that would stop me from being catapulted through the hatch above.

Arriving back at camp I checked with Fred and the map to find, to my consternation, that in the six months that I had been absent from 151 Alpha, because of commitments at other bases, there were now a number of roads that could no longer be driven over with any modicum of safety. Despite government reassurances to the contrary, the war was continuing to escalate and, with a sinking feeling, I realised that the terrorists were taking a stranglehold on the country. This feeling was reinforced the next day, when Roy and Jack reported seeing two ters, fleeing into the bush, while returning from deployment. With only an escort on the trucks no follow up could be contemplated.

The next day we headed for St. Barbara's mission. The trackers and follow up troops were within hours of their quarry and, if we could predict their forward movement, the gang might be apprehended.

St. Barbara's stood alone within craggy country dominated by granite hills and deep gorges. To get there we had to pass by St. Triashill mission, past the range of hills, where we had dropped off the arrogant Sergeant Major at the wrong point and where the Hyena had broken down and then past the place where I had picked up the body of a terrorist and on into the rugged scenery below.

So many memories returned as we crashed our way over the rough terrain. As we approached the mission, the church bell could be heard echoing across the valley. Our nerves were tense and emotions were running high. Why was the bell tolling? Was there a religious significance, or was it a warning that the security forces were coming?

Before the troop moved out in their continuing search, the priests were questioned closely. They denied any duplicity but our suspicions were not allayed and we left the troop leader still dissatisfied with the priest's explanations. Roy had accompanied me on this trip and as we returned he was in the leading Puma. Slowly we pulled out of the valley onto the open savannah above and, a few kilometres or so later we trundled slowly over an area of scrub where the track twisted and turned over two small culverts which, in the rainy season, would have had streams rushing below, before another steep climb towards St. Triashill mission.

Roy had almost reached the first culvert when, above the rattles and bangs of my truck, as it lurched over the bumps, I heard the unmistakable hollow boom of a mortar tube being fired. As Roy slowly negotiated the first culvert there was a report and a puff of smoke as the mortar detonated harmlessly ahead of him. Simultaneously, small arms fire opened up. The AK47's once again giving that strange rattling sound of pebbles on a corrugated iron roof which I had heard on my first call up at New Years Gift.

By now Roy was pulling hard up the hill ahead and the escorts were returning fire with sporadic shots as he lurched over the uneven ground. I could have stopped and we might have been safe, but we were in very open countryside and the voice of the instructor came quite clearly to me.

"It is dangerous to stop, so drive through the 'killing zone' because it is surprisingly difficult to hit a moving target."

I prayed that there were no landmines and selected second gear to take into account the bends and the climb ahead. As I approached the culverts I heard the sound of a second mortar being launched. I started counting the seconds off; eight seconds between launching and landing seemed to come to mind.

We were committed now and my foot was hard on the accelerator pedal. Just a few metres ahead, in the centre of the road, there was a flash and a thunderous report. We were so close to the explosion that the acrid smoke bellowed over the bonnet as we drove through the black cordite curtain. The small arms fire was rattling incessantly. The engine was screaming, the governor warning light was flashing with the buzzer angrily warning me, from the dashboard, that the diesel engine revs were rising to dangerous levels. There was a huge boom as another mortar exploded behind me; the smoke clearly visible through the rear view mirror. By now my escorts were returning fire from their precarious position on the back of my Puma.

Everything was happening so fast that my mind was in a whirl but, as I pulled myself together, I realised that I had heard no emergency call from Roy so, grabbing the handset, I yelled my call sign to 151 Alpha.

There was no immediate acknowledgement, but then Fred Mason's voice broke in.

"What's going on? Is there anybody hurt?" I put him in the picture as well as I could as we bumped up the hill and gave our location. He responded by ordering us back to camp - as if we had any intention of going anywhere else.

By now we were out of sight of the ambush and the firing had died away. We stopped to assess the damage and were very surprised to find very little. In fact, I have to admit that I felt slightly disappointed at the lack of evidence of the ordeal we had been through. I had noticed liquid spraying off Roy's Puma and had thought that the radiator had been hit but it turned out that both vehicles had received a hit on the water filled spare wheel carried on the rear. Other than a couple of ricochet marks on the steel plates where was no other damage. Despite the close proximity of the mortar explosion in front of me, there was no sign of any shrapnel marks. Our training to drive through an ambush was certainly vindicated. Moving targets were extremely hard to hit, although the mortar firing had been surprisingly accurate, with all three bombs straddling us on the road with the enemy's timing, fortunately for us, being just a few seconds out.

We set off again, but after less than a couple of kilometres a battered truck appeared driving towards us. It was not beyond the realms of possibility that the African driver was in league with the terrorists and was heading to pick them up so we stopped and searched the vehicle but, after questioning the driver, it became obvious that he was just delivering to a small general store that we had recently passed.

Just as we were about to let him go on his way, one of our escorts ran up excitedly, pointing at some thick bush.

"There are some people hiding in the bushes over there!"

We scrutinised the undergrowth and there definitely were some dark forms in the thicket. We scrambled for cover and then I shouted in English. "Come out!"

The shadowy heads bobbed about, but there was no response. I turned to one of my escorts.

"Tell them to come out or we will shoot," He shouted in shona, but there was still no acknowledgement. I felt reluctant to open fire in cold blood, but my escort had no such qualms. Before I could stop him he sent a burst from his machine gun thudding into the thicket.

Out jumped half a dozen black goats, none injured, bleating their protest as they rushed indignantly away. We looked at each other sheepishly and then burst into laughter as the tension released.

I found it difficult to concentrate on the drive back to camp. The adrenaline was pounding round my body. I was on a 'high' that no drug could simulate. Although I had flirted with danger on the race track for years, even being involved in a high speed pile up, I had never felt so exhilarated as I did now. To brush with near death or injury and escape unscathed must be the greatest feeling of elation there is. I felt then as though I had defied destiny.

I didn't feel so exhilarated however when, a few hours later, I was ordered back to the ambush point to pick up our troops who had completed a fruitless follow up. Fred was taking no chances though and, instead of our usual escort of a couple of troopies per vehicle armed with FN's, each Puma had four machine gunners. With the fire power of eight machine guns I couldn't help having just a tinge of hope that our assailants of that morning might be foolish enough to have a go at us again. It was, therefore, with a mixture of fear and trepidation that we stood in the dark evening shadows, beneath fir trees sighing in the wind, on the road back through St. Triashill mission awaiting the signal to proceed to the pick up point.

All went without incident however and a few hours later, back at camp, I lay on my bed unable to sleep, my mind going over the events of the day, still riding the wave of excitement.

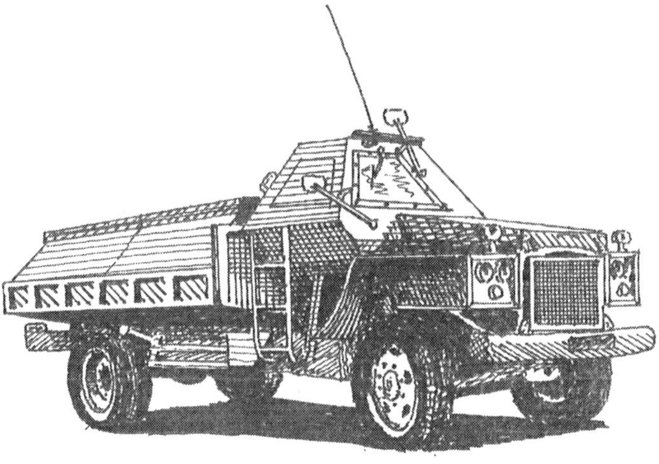

Puma

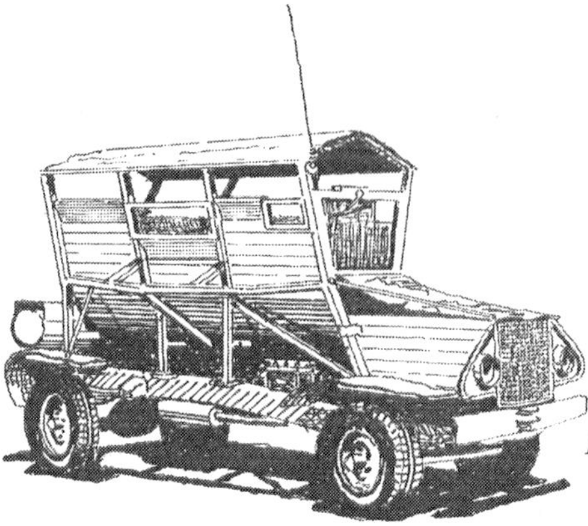

Hyena

CHAPTER 25

The Landmine

The abductors of Mr Christian had now moved out of our area and we had a couple of quiet days before being sent on a very grim mission.

151 Alpha had received a message that the pregnant wife and father of a local farmer had been killed when their car had struck a land mine. The farmer was away from home on call up with a mounted tracker unit involved in the follow up operations to find the abductors that we had come so close to catching.

Our job was to take a section officer into the Makoni area and locate the mounted unit where the officer had the unenviable task of conveying the dreadful news and of bringing the farmer back to Rusape.

Jack and I took two Hyenas and travelled north east to Bonda mission before we turned into an area totally unknown to us. It soon became very mountainous and barren and the darkening clouds overhead did nothing to relieve the tension which was slowly building up. What was even worse was that the information regarding the mounted unit's whereabouts was vague and inaccurate and we soon discovered that, despite having numerous maps, we had now left the area to which they referred. We had no option but to carry on blindly down the road when, after a kilometre as I negotiated a curve, I spied an object lying in the middle of the track some distance ahead. I immediately stopped and cautiously backed away. Checking with binoculars we could see that the object was a large canvas bag of the sort commonly used by Africans when travelling. It could be quite innocent, having dropped off the top of a bus or car but it could just as easily be an ambush or booby trap. One could never be too cautious in this situation because it wasn't unknown for terrorists to leave a booby-trapped transistor radio on the verge for some innocent civilian to pick it up.

The section officer was not taking any chances and we debussed and carried out a wide 360° sweep of the area before approaching the bag. Stealthily, one of the troopies checked for a booby trap and then gently tied a rope to the handles. From a safe distance it was pulled and jerked to reveal no booby traps.

Deciding, by now, that it was safe, we opened it up and searched the contents. It contained clothing, blankets, exercise books and food. The food consisted mainly of a high protein paste made from maize. The exercise books revealed a name and, from some of the writing, it appeared to belong to a young African going off to seek work. The bag had obviously fallen off a vehicle and one young man was going to be very disappointed when he reached his destination.

By now we were all tensed up so it was with dread and foreboding that, after a few more kilometres, we crested the edge of a long, deep valley. From our high point the road wound its way down between steep banks, so high in places that a grenade could have been dropped on top of us. On either side long saddles of mountainous grey granite overshadowed a stream that cut its way through thick vegetation on the valley floor.

During all of my call-ups I had never before witnessed a road twisting down into such a menacing and evil feeling place. Even my war hardened passengers gasped as I involuntarily stopped at the sight before us. I think we all had a premonition of a danger that we couldn't avoid.

Despite our deeply felt worries we couldn't call it a day and return to the camp because we were under orders to carry out this tragic task so, easing the Hyena over the crest, I had no option but to slow to a walking pace. The road was pock marked with land mine craters and, as we crossed and re-crossed the tumbling stream, we held our breath as we approached the narrow confines of each bridge. One bridge that crossed the stream, which by now was a torrent roaring down a rocky gorge, had even got a landmine crater half way across. The structure still seemed to be strong, but to avoid the hole meant scraping the raised concrete lip to get past. Slowly I moved across and as I gained the exit there was a deafening explosion. An object fell onto the road ahead, whilst debris hailed down on us.

My first thought was of an ambush, the Hyena seemed to be all right, so I accelerated hard up the slope ahead to stop out of sight on safer ground. We all scrambled out but by now it was quite evident that the following Hyena had disappeared.

As the thick dust cloud cleared we could make out the rear end upturned and half blocking the bridge, with the front of the wreck hanging at a crazy angle over the stream below. By chance, a large granite boulder, jutting out of the bank, had stopped the inevitable plunge into the gorge below. There was a deathly silence as we ran back, fearing for the victims trapped inside. They were still strapped in, dazed, but alive. We helped them out, all suffering from shock. Jack, being the driver and nearest the wheel which had detonated the explosion, was suffering from severe back pain. One of the medics checked him before we attempted to get him out. The bag which we had found was now a blessing in disguise as we could wrap everyone up in a blanket and soon we had some tea brewed.

While we sipped the hot liquid we had time to collect our thoughts and assess the situation. We couldn't retrace our steps to get assistance because the bridge was blocked by the hulk of the wrecked Hyena. We had no idea where the road ahead led to because we were some distance east of the maps we were carrying and, in any event, from its condition it would more than likely peter out after a few more kilometres. There was no response to our calls on the radios so it was decided that I would move my Hyena to higher ground and, as it had a more powerful radio, I would put out a 'mayday' call.

I had barely taken a couple of steps towards the vehicle when a shout went up. One of our escorts was pointing excitedly across the valley. In the distance we could see half a dozen villagers running from their huts into the dense foliage at the foot of the long granite saddle.

"They could have heard the explosion and be running away from us," commented the section officer. "On the other hand though, they could be alerting the ters to our predicament."

"Either way, a few shots in their direction won't go amiss."

A couple of volleys, fired at random, prompted the villagers to disappear even quicker into the undergrowth. We spread out a guard around our position and I continued on my way to call for help.

At first I could get no response but after what seemed an age, a reply crackled out of the loudspeaker. It was a radio station quite a long way away in the Inyanga mountains on a high plateau called 'Worlds View'. Using him as a relay I at last got a message through to 151 Alpha. Suddenly, through all the crackles and fade, the familiar voice of one of our radio operators came through loud and clear. It was a relief to talk to someone I knew. While I was explaining our situation Fred butted in and, although he was relieved to hear that there didn't appear to be any serious injuries, the airwaves got a bit blue when I could give no map reference to fix our position. Explanations would have to wait.

As there was no possibility of getting a helicopter into this hostile area, an army ambulance was dispatched with a Support Unit escort. We would have to try to talk them in from Bonda mission.

I retraced my steps and conveyed the good news to find that in my absence the section officer had established contact with the mounted tracker unit who were not far away and were making their way towards us.

"God, I hope the ambulance gets here before they do."

He looked tired and strained as he continued, "The poor bugger will flip his lid when he's told about his family, and we're stuck here."

The section officer was only in his twenties but he had the rank and the burden of responsibility weighing heavily on his young shoulders.

As if to add to our problems a single bark came from high above us, echoing between the granite buttresses.

"It's a baboon," answered a sergeant to my enquiring eyes.

"Mind you, the ters use animal calls as signals," adjoined one of the escorts mischievously. I took my position within our defensive circle.

The grey clouds that had been threatening us for so long, now released a heavy drizzle onto us. I crouched uncomfortably, water dripping off my cap, my clothes slowly soaking through. The occasional bark still echoed around us from the hills above.

We had a long time to wait and, in the comparative silence, my thoughts went back to my family and what the future held. What on earth was I doing in this hostile situation which was causing such disruption to our lives? Our government had conceded to African majority rule some years before and yet we were still fighting this insidious war. It was just turning into a vain attempt to keep some semblance of law and order whilst the warring factions of ZANU and ZAPU fought to gain a position of strength, almost as if it was a game of chess, except that we, the ordinary citizens, were the pawns. How much longer would it go on before they would all sit round a conference table to divide the spoils?

Morale in general, was getting very low and there had been some desertions from the unit. It was easy enough to just board a plane and leave the country. At that moment I was probably at my lowest ebb, which is the worst time to make a decision, but it was then that I decided that enough was enough. The writing had been on the wall for many years and we had chosen to ignore it. At one stage Vi and I had taken the step of finding out the cost of emigrating but, in the warm sunshine and pleasant life that we lived, we had stepped back from the decision. Many whites, including close friends had left to make new lives in various parts of the world. At thirty three years old I was getting too close to the age when I would find it harder and harder to get a job, raise a mortgage and the one hundred and one things needed to establish a new life elsewhere.

My thoughts were broken into by a radio call from the Hyena. The army ambulance had arrived at Bonda Mission and required directions to the dirt track that we had taken. We gazed dubiously in the opposite direction, but there was neither sight nor sound of horses or men. I was worried about Jack; the pain in his back was causing him considerable discomfort and he was suffering from shock. Despite rigging up a temporary shelter from a couple of ground sheets and giving him an extra blanket he was still cold and shivering. I felt guilty that I was annoyed when we first met at Tomlinson Depot, but I wouldn't have wished this sort of introduction to Support Unit on anyone. We brewed some more tea and continued to wait. The baboons were now quiet and the drizzle had relented. A watery sun broke through the clouds and slowly started to dry us out.

The radio signals from the ambulance party were getting stronger the closer they approached but by now we had received a message from the tracker unit. They had us visual and would be arriving shortly and, in fact, within a few minutes they came into view. Not only was it a unit of about five horsemen but shuffling behind was a group of locals who were obviously being held for questioning.

Our Section Officer took their Patrol Leader to one side and explained our reason for being there. They would all have been farmers from the same area and he looked shocked as he heard the news. A tall, well built man was called over, his rifle surreptitiously removed and, as he heard the facts, he gave a great bellow of rage and distress. I felt a lump in my throat as tears pricked my eyes. I looked away, feeling like an intruder at this moment of personal grief. Then this massive man crumpled and collapsed, sobbing and crying out in anguish. I walked away, unable to endure the pain that enveloped the air.

There was a sudden commotion as, in his despair and anger,he leapt at the group of prisoners as if to avenge his personal tragedy. His comrades pulled him back before he could give physical vent to his feelings and he again collapsed, sobbing quietly to himself, like a heartbroken child.

The sound of a vehicle approaching broke the wretchedness of the moment and thankfully a Support Unit Puma appeared, negotiating the narrow track, with the ambulance close behind. Our relief was unbounded. The medics took the distressed farmer into the ambulance where he was sedated and our injured troops were soon tucked up on the stretchers within.

A rope was then attached to the wrecked Hyena which was dragged along the parapet by the Puma until it ignominiously toppled over into the gorge and water below.

Other than the two large craters on the roadway, the bridge structure appeared to be sound and it was with great relief that I drove my Hyena back over the bridge and, in sombre mood, followed the sad convoy out of the desolate valley.

A day or two later, which was a Sunday, Fred came looking for a driver to take two African troopies into Salisbury. I was lucky enough to draw the short straw and we were soon on our way.

Passing through Rusape, I took the opportunity of stopping at the hospital to check on the progress of Jack and the other troopies injured in the land mine blast. Fortunately the x rays had revealed no long term damage and, although they were still in pain, they only had severe bruising.

My next stop was the public telephone at the Balfour Hotel.

"Lay another place for lunch," I told Vi, and she whooped with delight.

The mine protected Land Rover could just about reach 120 kph and I kept my foot flat to the floor boards all the way. After dropping off my passengers at Tomlinson Depot I hurried on home. Vi and the kids were delighted at my unexpected appearance and soon I was tucking into the Sunday roast.

It was not all fun though, as we took the opportunity to have a serious talk about emigrating, my mind being completely made up. At about the same time as we had closed our business, when we had previously talked about emigrating, Vi and I had made a conscious decision to liquidate all our fixed assets, so we had sold our house and had moved into rented accommodation. The reasoning behind this being that, with the situation as it was, we wanted to be in a position to either leave quickly, once a decision had been taken, or to have the cash to start again if we decided to stay. Now we decided that, first thing on Monday morning Vi would start the ball rolling to get all the paperwork completed as quickly as possible.

All too soon I had to wave goodbye again to the family and, a little later than I had planned, I started the 200 kilometre trek back to camp. It was about 5.00 p.m. as I approached Macheke, which was about half way and, being the beginning of winter, the sun was getting low and the light diminishing. Realising that I had not seen another vehicle for some time and twilight was a very dangerous time to be driving, I cocked my rifle and laid it across the passenger seat to cover the countryside rushing by. I was also armed with a 9 mm Browning pistol which I removed from its holster, cocked and laid at the ready to fire if necessary.

It was very nerve-wracking as the dusk drew in and it was with great relief that I eventually saw the lights of Rusape in the distance. A short while later I turned into the protection of the base camp.

The abductors were now well out of our operational area and the hunt was handed over to another unit. Fred was in a vile mood and I think what annoyed him most was that, every time he looked at the large wall map in the ops room, the only contacts or sightings of the enemy in recent weeks were by us drivers. None of the highly trained troops, operating observation posts and tracker units, had got anywhere. It was a personal humiliation for him to have this gang running rings around us. Mind you, it was not an easy task tracking ters over the mountainous countryside in which we operated. The areas were vast and our security forces ill equipped. Trade sanctions certainly did affect our ability to fight this war. If we had had more helicopters and therefore been able to deploy faster, our success rate would have been much higher.

For the rest of this call up my nerves were on edge every time that I left the confines of the camp and, one night, I had to take the lead truck to deploy India troop. We drove into the Makoni and towards the crater pocked road of a few days earlier. Peering through the small bullet proof windscreen, the gloom was suddenly penetrated by a flash of light, followed by a muffled explosion. It was in the direction in which we were travelling, but some distance ahead. I was convinced that we were heading into trouble and, at one stage, found that I was so nervous that I had unconsciously slowed to a walking pace. It was a cold night, but I was sweating profusely. Eventually I stopped close to the drop off point. The flashes were getting steadily brighter and the explosions louder.

"God, I'm glad to get off," said the Troop Leader thankfully. "This truck is a sitting target."

It turned out that the troop were also worried about the explosions and were as nervous as me. As they melted into the night we turned with relief and headed back to camp.

We never did find out what caused those explosions. It was dismissed as being an electric storm in the granite hills although I had never seen lightning in May before, as it is a cold, dry month with little in the way of storms. There were rumours however that it was a skirmish between two different terrorist factions, but this was never confirmed.

When the time came for me to leave I surveyed the camp with mixed feelings. Despite the problems of this call up, previously there had been some good times and many laughs. In adversity one makes some very good friends and, although I hoped never to see the place again, I felt a tinge of sadness as a chapter in my life closed.

Two months later, in August 1978, I arrived in Britain to set up home for my family, who followed shortly afterwards, and to start a new life.

*

This had been a war involving not only the military, but people from all walks of life. There were the Africans, caught in the middle, intimidated, maimed and murdered by the terrorists, and interrogated and scared of the security forces. A people like any other, who only wanted to carry on their traditional lifestyles in peace.

There were the white farmers in the front line, armed wherever they went, with their families at risk and their work force in danger of being murdered and their houses burned to the ground.

There were the white 'townies' called up in their thousands from seventeen years old to sixty. All our lives were disrupted, our jobs, businesses and careers in danger, let alone the risks involved on call up duty. You were just as likely to bump into your bank manager as you were an old school friend. In the end everyone had a commitment, even those physically unable to carry out normal army duties.

We all had a commitment to fight the war and, at the same time, earn a living to pay the bills. Civilians are, unfortunately, always caught up in any war, but in this war a large number of the security forces were part timers.